Imperialism's New Clothes

American University Studies

Series IX
History
Vol. 79

PETER LANG
New York • Bern • Frankfurt am Main • Paris

Brian Digre

Imperialism's New Clothes

The Repartition of Tropical Africa, 1914-1919

PETER LANG
New York • Bern • Frankfurt am Main • Paris

Library of Congress Cataloging-in-Publication Data

Digre, Brian Kenneth
   Imperialism's new clothes : the repartition of tropical
Africa, 1914-1919 / Brian Digre.
      p. cm. — (American university studies. Series IX,
History ; vol. 79)
      Includes bibliographical references.
      1. World War, 1914-1918 — Territorial questions —
Africa.   2. Africa — Politics and government — To 1945.
3. Africa — Colonization.   4. World War, 1914-1918 —
Africa.   I. Title   II. Series.
D651.A4D54   1990   940.3'1424 — dc20   89-28908
ISBN 0-8204-1120-5   CIP
ISSN 0740-0462

CIP-Titelaufnahme der Deutschen Bibliothek

Digre, Brian:
Imperialism's new clothes : the repartition of
tropical Africa; 1914—1919 / Brian Digre. —
New York; Bern; Frankfurt am Main; Paris:
Lang, 1990.
   (American University Studies: Ser. 9,
   History; Vol. 79)
   ISBN 0-8204-1120-5

NE: American University Studies / 09

© Peter Lang Publishing, Inc., New York 1990

Printed by Weihert-Druck GmbH, Darmstadt, West Germany

To my father, Kenneth S. Digre

Contents

Maps

Abbreviations

AGR	Archives Générales du Royaume, Brussels
AMAE,B	Archives du Ministère des Affaires Etrangères, Brussels
Af	Collection Afrique
AMAE,F	Archives du Ministère des Affaires Etrangères, Paris
ANSOM	Archives Nationales, Section Outre-Mer, Paris
AP	Fonds Affaires Politiques
BLO	Bodleian Library, Oxford
FRUS	U.S. Department of State. *Papers Relating to the Foreign Relations of the United States, The Paris Peace Conference, 1919*, 13 vols. Washington, D.C.: Government Printing Office, 1942-47
HLRO	House of Lords Record Office, London
NA	National Archives, Washington, D.C.
PRO	Public Record Office, Kew
CAB	Cabinet Papers
CO	Colonial Office Papers
FO	Foreign Office Papers

Preface

The First World War was a watershed event in the history of European colonialism in Africa. A major repartition of colonial empires occurred as a result. It was the war, and the peace conference following it, that gave birth to the mandate system of the League of Nations. For millions of Africans the conflict also meant untold suffering in a conflict not their own.

This book is primarily a diplomatic history of Allied designs on Germany's colonies in tropical Africa. It examines the motives that drove Britain, France and Belgium to conquer and divide Togo, Cameroon and German East Africa between 1914 and 1919. In the process, it explores the Allied argument that a colonial redivision of the continent corresponded with African desires.

Fine studies by William Roger Louis, Christopher M. Andrew and A.S. Kanya-Forstner assess imperialism during the period from the national perspectives of Britain and France. The comparative international approach adopted here both expands and concentrates the topic. It explores the relationships of the nations' policies and uses the materials available in the different countries' archives to shed further light on the objectives pursued by the others. At the same time, the study remains closely focused on the three German colonies in tropical Africa. Togo, Cameroon and German East Africa were regarded as sharing common characteristics, and they were grouped together in 1919 to form the B category of mandates.

Outside of tropical Africa, responsibility for the conquest of Germany's colonies lay with Japan and the British Dominions. German Southwest Africa is the one German colony in Africa that falls outside the primary scope of this study. From the beginning of the war until the end of the peace conference the Allies treated the colony as though it were in the Union of

South Africa's sphere of influence. Expansionist South African attitudes had much in common with those of policy makers in Australia and New Zealand. Indeed, at the peace conference German Southwest Africa would be joined with Germany's former colonies in the Pacific to create the C mandates.

The foreign policy of the United States does enter into the picture. American participation was of crucial importance in developing the mandate system and its application to central Africa. The related issue of supposed African preferences is dealt with in detail. At the end of the war and during the peace conference, Allied leaders advanced the altruistic public position that confiscating Germany's colonies corresponded with the desires of the colonies' inhabitants. This argument has long been viewed as the product of self-serving Allied propaganda. My research on the issue reveals the divergence of public and private positions. It also illustrates the existence of African opinions at odds with the postwar settlement and the awareness of British decision makers that they were sacrificing African concerns even as they claimed to protect them.

I would like to express my appreciation for the assistance I received from the archivists, and for permission to quote from the documents, at the Public Record Office in Kew, the House of Lords Record Office in London, the Bodleian Library in Oxford, the Archives du Ministère des Affaires Etrangères and the Archives Nationales, Section Outre-Mer in Paris, the Archives du Ministère des Affaires Etrangères and the Archives Générales du Royaume in Brussels and the National Archives and the Library of Congress in Washington, D.C. Quotations from the Harcourt Manuscripts and confidential correspondence of Philip Kerr appear with the kind permission of the Hon. Mrs. Crispin Gascoigne and the Marquis of Lothian. I also wish to thank the University of Southern Mississippi for its financial support, Karolyn S. Thompson for help in obtaining materials, Jean Gates for technical assistance and Christopher Guidroz for drawing the maps.

Some of my research has been presented in papers at meetings of the French Colonial Historical Society and the African Studies Association. I am grateful for the resulting suggestions and for the comments of those who have read the manuscript. I owe a special debt to Charles Herber for his encouragement and advice. Most particularly I wish to thank Laurie Evans for her counsel and critical reading of the manuscript. The shortcomings are naturally my own.

1

The Struggle For Tropical Africa

The War's Swift Spread to Africa: August 1914

Using history as a guide, one should not be surprised by the decision to fight a European war in Africa. During the eighteenth and nineteenth centuries, wars between European states regularly spread to other places in the world. Nevertheless, there was a cruel irony in the fighting that began in Africa in 1914. Among the altruistic reasons advanced in support of European imperialism had been the contention that it would end ethnic warfare in Africa. Now Africans were called upon to kill each other because of a conflict between European states.

The African minister John Chilembwe, who would lead a wartime revolt against British rule in Nyasaland, aptly summarized this humanitarian argument against the spread of the war to Africa. In a letter to the *Nyasaland Times* in late 1914, he wrote: "On the commencement of the war we understood that it was said indirectly that Africa had nothing to do with the civilised war. But now we find that the poor African has already been plunged into the great war."[1]

With regard to a large part of central Africa, this position also had a basis in international law. Britain, France, Belgium

---

[1] George Shepperson and Thomas Price, *Independent African: John Chilembwe and the Origins, Setting and Significance of Nyasaland Native Rising of 1915* (Edinburgh: Edinburgh University Press, 1958), p. 234.

and Germany were signatories of the Berlin Act of 1885. The act had created a free trade zone, known as the conventional basin of the Congo, which included a vast section of central Africa from five degrees north latitude to the Zambezi River. Under the Berlin Act the colonial powers by common consent could maintain the neutrality of this region.[2]

The perception of military exigencies thrust aside these humanitarian and legal peacetime rationales. Without consideration of the long-term consequences for Africa, the war was extended to the continent. The British decided to strike at Germany in areas where Britain was stronger and where they perceived strategic threats. Given the precipitate nature of the events in the early days of the war, the initial decisions of the Western European statesmen should be viewed as preliminary to, rather than as integral parts of, their wartime colonial objectives. Yet their actions did reflect future developments in their colonial policies.

Tropical Africa was not, in any case, the principal concern of Western European leaders in August 1914. The rapid German advance in the West threatened France, Belgium and Britain with decisive defeat. Quite naturally the decision makers in these countries were preoccupied with the cascading course of events on the western front. On August 3, Germany declared war on France. During the night German troops began their sweep through Belgium, and on the fourth Britain declared war on Germany. As their stunning advance proceeded, the German troops pushed aside the Belgian forces and drove deep into northern France. They were stopped before Paris only in the crucial Battle of the Marne, which raged from the fifth to the twelfth of September.

---

[2] R.C. Hawkin, "The Belgian Proposal to Neutralise Central Africa during the European War," *Problems of the War: Papers read before the Grotius Society in the Year 1915*, Vol. 1 (London: Sweet and Maxwell, 1916), appendix p. 75.

As these events were unfolding, the Belgians made a well-documented attempt to maintain the neutrality of at least the Belgian Congo. On August 7 the Belgian minister of foreign affairs, Viscount Julien Davignon, dispatched telegrams with this aim to his ministers in Paris and London. His message began, "Belgium trusts that the war will not be extended to Central Africa. The Governor of the Belgian Congo has received instructions to maintain a strictly defensive attitude."[3] Davignon then requested that inquiries be made of the British and French governments regarding what they intended to do in the conventional basin of the Congo. A telegram later the same day from Davignon to his ministers reconfirmed his position. It stated, "In view of the civilising mission common to colonising nations, the Belgian Government desire, in effect, for humanitarian reasons not to extend the field of hostilities to Central Africa."[4]

The initial French and British replies deferred making a decision on the proposal. Baron Paul Guillaume, the Belgian minister in Paris, reported the following day on a conversation he had with President Raymond Poincaré of France. Poincaré promised to discuss the matter with his colonial minister and noted that his first impression was that "he could see little difficulty in proclaiming the neutrality of the French Congo, but he nevertheless reserves his reply." Poincaré added that fighting might already have broken out on the Ubangui.[5] On August 14 M. de Lalaing, Belgian minister in London, replied to Davignon in a similar fashion. He reported that the Foreign Office had not yet reached a decision on this question, which

---

[3] Belgium, Ministère des Affaires Etrangères, *Diplomatic Correspondence respecting The War* (London: His Majesty's Stationery Office, 1914), pp. 53-54.

[4] Ibid., pp. 54-55.

[5] Ibid., pp. 55-56 and "Davignon au Ministre des colonies" August 11, 1914, Collection Afrique, Af 1/2, Archives du Ministère des Affaires Etrangères, Brussels (AMAE,B).

they considered extremely delicate, and would tell him only that the situation was being studied.[6]

Actually, British plans were advancing more rapidly than de Lalaing appeared to realize. Early in August a joint naval and military subcommittee of the Committee of Imperial Defence had been formed to consider joint expeditions. The subcommittee included members of the Admiralty, Colonial Office, War Office and India Office and military representatives of the colonial armed forces. On August 5 the subcommittee reached conclusions which included the following:

> ... an expedition should be sent from India against Dar-es-Salaam.
>
> The Sub-Committee believed that by the reduction of this *point d'appui* of the German naval forces off the coast of East Africa the Admiralty arrangements for the protection of commerce would be facilitated, and that by thus taking the offensive the defence of the British possessions in East Africa would be best guaranteed....
>
> [In West Africa, provided the local military situation allowed] ... it was highly desirable that the British forces in the Gold Coast Colony, reinforced if possible from Sierra Leone, should be used for offensive purposes against Togoland, with a view to destroying the wireless telegraph stations in that Colony.[7]

British operations in Cameroon and German Southwest Africa were viewed as requiring more careful planning, and it was recommended that the beginning of military operations

---

[6] De Lalaing to Davignon, London, August 14, 1914, Af 1/2, AMAE,B.

[7] "Proceedings of a Sub-committee of the Committee of Imperial Defence, August 5, 1914," Harcourt Papers, 508:6, Bodleian Library, Oxford (BLO).

there be postponed. The cabinet approved these recommendations on August 6.[8] Thus, only two days after declaring war on Germany, the British government sanctioned the commencement of hostilities in Africa.

The quotation from the subcommittee's report shows that the group initially was concerned with military strategy. Ensuring British control of the seas was the principal aim. To accomplish this, two measures in particular needed to be carried out. First, German wireless stations, which were capable of relaying information to German ships in the South Atlantic and the Indian Ocean, had to be captured or destroyed. In German East Africa this could be accomplished by a naval raid on Dar es Salaam, while in West Africa it compelled the British to undertake a land campaign to capture the powerful German transmitter located at Kamina, in the interior of Togo. The second military task required attacks upon German colonial ports to deny bases to German commerce raiders.

The French government was quite willing to adhere to the colonial military option favored by the British. In fact, the French seemed eager to participate in the proposed military campaigns. In a dispatch to the French ambassador in London on August 10, the French Foreign Ministry official Pierre de Margerie wrote that he had spoken with the British ambassador about joint operations in Cameroon. The British ambassador had announced that Britain intended to occupy Duala and inquired whether the French desired to collaborate in the action. De Margerie responded that France was ready to participate in occupying the port, as well as other ports, and proposed that in addition France should occupy areas of Cameroon bordering on French Equatorial Africa.[9] On August

---

[8] Ibid., 508:6, 7, 28 and 302.

[9] Telegram (draft), de Margerie to the French ambassador in London, August 10, 1914, "Possessions allemandes d'Afrique II, Opérations militaires franco-britanniques 1914 Août-Déc.," 1545, La Série Guerre 1914-1918, Archives du Ministère des Affaires Etrangères, Paris (AMAE,F).

16 these French intentions were confirmed in a report to Davignon by the Belgian minister in Paris. Describing a conversation with de Margerie on colonial affairs, he reported:

> M. de Margerie considered that in view of the present situation Germany should be attacked wherever possible; he believes that such is also the opinion of Great Britain, who certainly has claims to satisfy; France wishes to get back that part of the Congo which she has been compelled to give up in consequence of the Agadir incident.[10]

Any Belgian hopes that some conditions of peace could have been maintained in central Africa must have disappeared with the report from de Lalaing in London on August 17. He stated that the British government could not accept the Belgian proposal for the neutrality of the conventional basin of the Congo. Without indicating who had initiated the conflict, he reported that fighting had broken out in East Africa, with the Germans attacking the British Central African Protectorate and the British attacking Dar es Salaam. "In these circumstances, the British Government, even if they were convinced from the political and strategical point of view of the utility of the Belgian proposal, would be unable to adopt it."[11]

As these diplomatic exchanges were taking place, discussions concerning the Congo's neutrality were going on within the Belgian government. The immediate problem was that the government desired to cooperate militarily with Britain and France in Africa while not abandoning with unseemly haste the neutrality of its colony. The dilemma was described as early as August 7 by Pierre Orts, a Belgian diplomat who

---

[10] Belgium, *Diplomatic Correspondence*, p. 68 and Guillaume to Davignon, August 16, 1914, Af 1/2, AMAE,B.

[11] Belgium, *Diplomatic Correspondence*, pp. 68-69 and de Lalaing to Davignon, August 17, 1914, Af 1/2, AMAE,B.

would play a leading role in developing Belgium's colonial war aims. In a note to the colonial minister he argued that two things had changed since the conditions of neutrality had been sent by the Belgian government to the Congo on July 30: Belgium and Germany were now at war, and military cooperation existed between Belgium and the Western powers. Thus, he concluded it was no longer possible to maintain complete neutrality. On August 6 the Congo's governor general had been advised of Allied military cooperation and requested not to apply the rules of neutrality to British, French and Russian naval vessels. About these directions Orts now advised, "it appears that we are obliged to maintain the instructions sent yesterday to the Governor General under pain of placing ourselves in the most false position, vis a vis our Allies."[12]

The Belgians, however, did seek recompense for their cooperation. Bending the rules of the Congo's neutrality would heighten the possibility that the colony would be treated as a bargaining chip in a peace settlement. Hence the Belgian government sought an Allied guarantee of its sovereignty over the Congo. This position was accurately described in a dispatch to the British foreign secretary, Sir Edward Grey, by the British ambassador to Belgium, Sir F.H. Villiers, on August 22, 1914. Villiers summarized "somewhat lengthy discussions" which had taken place between him, the secretary general of the Belgian Foreign Ministry and the French ambassador. He concluded:

> The result is that the Belgian Government are prepared to afford to their allies such facilities as they may require for military operations in W. Africa, asking in return for assurances that Great Britain and France will support them in securing

---

[12] "Note pour Monsieur le Ministre des Colonies," August 7, 1914, Af 1/2, AMAE,B.

the independence and integrity of their colonial possessions.[13]

At this point, with the Allies having decided on an extension of the fighting beyond Europe, Germany made a belated attempt to neutralize its central African colonies. On August 23, 1914, Germany appealed to the United States to intercede under the Berlin Act to ensure the neutrality of the conventional basin of the Congo. The United States replied that since the Senate had not ratified the Berlin Act it could not so intervene. It did agree to serve as a means of communication to the Allies.[14]

This German diplomatic initiative had no real potential for preventing warfare in Africa. Britain was determined to attack Germany's colonies for military reasons from the outset of hostilities in Europe. France was more than willing to cooperate in this enterprise, and Belgium had little choice or desire to do anything but cooperate with its European supporters. The way was opened for four years of killing in Africa, accompanied by new visions of imperialist expansion. The result was a colonial repartition of the continent.

German Colonialism and Tropical Africa: Myths and Realities

Eventual Allied victory would make Germany's colonies the subject of this new burst of imperialism in Africa. Germany had acquired its colonies rapidly during the 1880s. Differing

---

[13] Draft of letter to Sir Edward Grey, August 22, 1914, "Neutrality of the Congo/Attitude of Belgium," (Note states that the draft was lent to the Belgians by Villiers on May 29, 1916), Af 1/2, AMAE,B.

[14] Mary Townsend, *The Rise and Fall of Germany's Colonial Empire 1884-1918* (New York: Macmillan Co., 1930), p. 364 and Hawkin, "Supplementary Note," p. 84.

greatly in size, population, geography and climate, the colonies formed a disparate collection.

Togo, the smallest, was a thin inland projection from the West African coast. On the eve of the war, its African population numbered one million, but it had only 327 German residents.[15]

Cameroon, a far larger colony with an African population of 2,650,000 and 1,311 Germans, covered a varied terrain.[16] Mangrove swamps along the coast gave way to rain forests in the interior. Near the Nigerian border, Mount Cameroon rose to more than 13,000 feet. Situated on the mountain's slopes, the town of Buea had a temperate climate, coveted by Europeans as a place where they could recover from the tropical environment below and where European vegetables and dairy products could be produced.[17] Beyond the coastal plain rose a central plateau. In the higher northern portion, the plateau turned into grasslands. The southern part merged into the tropical rain forest of the Congo basin.

German East Africa was Germany's largest colony, and its indigenous population of 7,500,000 was greater than that

---

[15] Arthur J. Knoll, *Togo Under Imperial Germany 1884-1914* (Stanford: Hoover Institution Press, 1978), p. 91. The African population figures given here and for the following colonies are estimated. The German figures are for 1911 and are found in L.H. Gann and Peter Duignan, *The Rulers of German Africa 1884-1914* (Stanford: Stanford University Press, 1977), p. 241. This source also is used for the German populations of the other African colonies.

[16] Harry R. Rudin, *Germans in the Cameroons 1884-1914* (New Haven: Yale University Press, 1938; reprint edition, Hamden, Conn.: Archon Books, 1968), p. 102.

[17] Ibid., pp. 103-106. There are several possible spelling variations for Cameroon and its port, Duala. In the text the foregoing are used; in direct quotations the original spellings have been retained.

of all Germany's other colonies combined.[18] Along the coast an equatorial climate supported tropical vegetation. In much of the interior, however, inadequate rainfall and wide areas infested with the tsetse fly made agriculture and cattle-raising difficult or impossible. Almost half the population lived in the northwestern territories of Ruanda and Urundi.[19] There the naturally fertile soils of the western rift highlands made the dense population possible. In the entire colony the German population numbered only 3,113.

These three colonies in tropical Africa differed in several ways from German Southwest Africa. The latter had the largest German population, 11,140 settlers, and the smallest number of African inhabitants, 208,000.[20] Despite the colony's arid climate and the Namib Desert which stretched inland from the dangerous Atlantic coast, it was viewed as a potential colony of settlement. The central highlands contained fine cattle-raising areas, and the dispossession and killing of the African inhabitants of the region in the early twentieth century opened limited opportunities for German immigrants.

To most German colonial enthusiasts these territories appeared relatively small and geographically separated when compared with the colonial acquisitions of Britain, France and Belgium in Africa. Consequently, the Germans sought to increase the size of their African possessions, primarily but not exclusively at the expense of Belgium and Portugal. Germans also coveted French territories, particularly French Equatorial

---

[18] William O. Henderson, *Studies in German Colonial History* (Chicago: Quadrangle Books, 1962), p. 87.

[19] William Roger Louis, *Ruanda-Urundi 1884-1919* (Oxford: Clarendon Press, 1963), p. 109. These feudal African states have become the republics of Rwanda and Burundi. For consistency, I refer to them as Ruanda and Urundi, the colonial terms used in the early 1900s.

[20] Eric A. Walker, *A History of Southern Africa* (London: Longmans, 1957), p. 593. The African population estimate is for the territory at the end of the First World War.

Africa. Although at times bellicose in their demands, German statesmen generally were willing to see this expansion achieved in a manner which would have accommodated British interests.

German foreign policy in the prewar years clearly illustrates these colonial objectives. They were evident, for example, in the Moroccan Crisis of 1911. In that year the new German foreign minister, Alfred von Kiderlen-Wächter, challenged the expansion of French authority in Morocco. Kiderlen's principal objective was to acquire all of French Equatorial Africa as compensation.[21]

The crisis ended in a negotiated settlement, which created a new source of Franco-German conflict in central Africa. Although the German foreign minister did not gain all he wanted, France was forced to cede parts of French Equatorial Africa. To the French colonial party this concession became the source of both bitterness arising from the loss and apprehension about future German aims. In addition, Germany's agreement to respect the rights of concessionary companies operating in the newly acquired areas proved the source of continuing quarrels between German and French economic interests.

---

[21] Ernst Jaeckh, *Kiderlen-Wächter*, vol. 2, pp. 128ff, quoted in Fritz Fischer, *War of Illusions: German Policies from 1911 to 1914*, trans. Mariam Jackson (New York: W.W. Norton and Co., 1975), p. 76. Fischer discusses the crisis in detail, revealing the complexity of German motives. French resistance to German ambitions led to increased European tensions. Here the Kaiser drew back, and Kiderlen offered his resignation. In making the offer Kiderlen stated the rationale behind his policy:

> We must have the whole of the French Congo – this is the last opportunity without taking up arms – of obtaining something useful in Africa. Attractive bits of Congo with rubber and ivory are of no use to us; we must get as far as the Belgian Congo so that we are there if it is carved up and so that, as long as this structure exists, we obtain access through it to our East Africa.

In contrast to the antagonism engendered by the conflicting aims of French and German imperialism, British and German prewar colonial policies in Africa appeared to contain greater leeway for accommodation. Perhaps this was because the bargaining chips were primarily other nations' colonies. Although conversations on the issue seem to contradict the growing tensions between Britain and Germany, they nevertheless represent an area in which certain British official circles were willing to consider concessions in the hope of satisfying German ambitions and improving relations.[22]

Negotiations along these lines did take place between the two countries. Beginning in 1911 and continuing until 1914, the discussions focused on the African colonies of Portugal and Belgium. These conversations envisioned dividing the smaller states' colonies into German and British economic spheres of interest. They also considered the prospect of partitioning Angola, Mozambique and the Belgian Congo.[23] Despite these negotiations, concrete results failed to materialize. In 1914,

---

[22] From the British perspective an illustration of this attitude can be seen in a letter from the British colonial secretary, Lewis Harcourt, to Sir John Anderson. Requesting Anderson's opinion on the exchange of territory with Germany in Africa, Harcourt wrote:

> I think you know that I have had it in my mind for some time that Anglo-German relations could be permanently improved if we had "conversations" leading to exchanges of territory which might give Germany a "place in the sun" without injury to our Colonial or Imperial interests...The "deal" – if there is one – , should be rather to the advantage of Germany – at least there should be no ground for saying that we had "done" her.

Lewis Harcourt to John Anderson, December 12, 1911, Harcourt Papers, 496:173-174, BLO.

[23] Fischer, *War of Illusions*, pp. 310-319.

German colonial enthusiasts quickly transformed their prewar territorial objectives into war aims.

The existence of Anglo-German discussions also had implications for Allied wartime colonial policy. First, they indicate that before the war the British were willing to accept limited German colonial expansion in Africa. Changes in this British attitude, therefore, require explanations. Second, the sincerity of British wartime accusations against German colonial rule demand careful evaluation. In addition, Belgian suspicion of British intentions naturally was heightened when the Belgians gained knowledge of the prewar talks.

Beyond the diplomacy of European imperialism, three other areas of German colonial policy – militarization, native policy and economic value – proved to be topics of considerable debate during the war and the peace conference. Sketching the reality of German colonialism in these fields offers a basis for evaluating Allied wartime assertions.

During the war there were frequent charges that the Germans either had militarized their colonies or would do so in the future. Despite images of Prussian militarism in Africa, the German colonies had among the smallest military establishments on the continent. Rudin's detailed study of German rule in Cameroon provides firm evidence of the colony's non-threatening posture.[24] Although relatively stronger militarily in German East Africa, the Germans were considerably weaker in Togo.[25] Only in German Southwest Africa were there sizable European forces, but these were no match for the much larger

---

[24] Rudin, *Germans in the Cameroons 1884-1914*, p. 195. "In 1914 there were about 1200 police officered by 30 whites; the troops numbered 1550 in 1914 and their officers 185. Both figures are so small that it is ridiculous to assert that the Germans militarized their colony," observes the author.

[25] Further support for this appraisal of German military strength can be found in its comparison with other European colonial forces in Gann and Duignan, *The Rulers of German Africa 1884-1914*, p. 106.

number of troops available in the neighboring Union of South Africa.[26] The Germans had no fortified naval bases in Africa.

In the field of native policy, the wartime statements of Western leaders and corresponding press accounts stigmatized German colonial rule because of its mistreatment of Africans. Early German colonial rule was certainly harsh. The suppressions of the Maji Maji Rebellion of 1905 in German East Africa and especially of the Herero Rising of 1904-07 in German Southwest Africa stand as odiously brutal chapters in the African colonial experience. Charges of widespread and frequent whippings of Africans also were essentially accurate.

In spite of such facts, an objective evaluation differs from the wartime accusations for several reasons. Western charges failed to compare German rule with the policies of other colonial powers. Without in any way dismissing the often barbarous nature of German rule, it is necessary to view it in the overall context of European colonialism in Africa, which was often no better.

Nor did Allied wartime propaganda of the legendary brutality of the Germans give much consideration to the role Africans played in the dynamics of colonialism. The idea that other colonial powers were more humane is rejected by M. Semakula Kiwanuka. "This concept is of course a myth, because the response of each colonial power was conditioned by the extent of the challenge or the degree of collaboration by the Africans."[27]

There is also a distinguishable pattern in the policies pursued by most of the European colonial powers in Africa. Usually the colonial policies moved from initial conquest and suppression of opposition to an increasing focus on economic devel-

---

[26] Byron Farwell, *The Great War in Africa, 1914-1918* (New York: W.W. Norton and Co., 1986), p. 75.

[27] M. Semakula Kiwanuka, "Colonial Policies and Administrations in Africa: The Myths of the Contrasts," *African Historical Studies* 2 (1970):296.

opment. In general, it was after the First World War that the latter policies gained their greatest prominence. Consequently, in comparison with the other colonial powers, German colonial rule in Africa was concentrated in the initial and usually more brutal stages of modern imperialism.

Even during this period the negative aspects of German colonialism were not impervious to reform. Following the appointment of Bernhard Dernburg as colonial minister in 1906, the Germans made efforts to correct some of the worst abuses. For example, reforms were introduced into the system of compulsory labor. Also in some areas, such as scientific research against tropical diseases, the Germans made important contributions.

The economics of German colonialism produced considerable controversy at the peace conference and thereafter. The Allies dismissed the economic value of the colonies to Germany, while the Germans sought to counter their arguments.

Germany's major colonies failed to balance their budgets before the war and required subsidies. According to figures cited by Gann and Duignan, these government subsidies totaled 451.5 million marks between 1884 and 1914. Of this amount more than half (278 million) went to Southwest Africa, where the cost of military campaigns proved a significant expense. East Africa received most of what remained (122 million), with 48 million marks being spent in Cameroon and 3.5 million in Togo.[28] Only in Togo, sometimes called "the model colony," did government revenues regularly exceed expenditures. There a frugal colonial administration frequently was able to draw sufficient funds from import duties, direct taxes and railroad and wharf receipts.[29]

---

[28] Figures from H. Schnee, ed., *Deutsches Kolonial-Lexikon*, 3 vols., cited by Gann and Duignan, *The Rulers of German Africa*, appendix E, table E. 2, p. 257.

[29] Knoll, *Togo Under Imperial Germany 1884-1914*, pp. 73-79.

Emigration from Germany to its colonies never really flourished. As a result, an increasing emphasis was placed on the commercial value of the colonies during the years before the war. German colonial promoters argued that the colonies would provide Germany with secure supplies of raw materials. In both Togo and Cameroon palm oil exports were important. In Togo colonial promoters made an ambitious attempt to encourage cotton production, but it failed to achieve the hoped-for results.

During the early twentieth century, Germans relied upon the concessionary company system to exploit rubber resources in south Cameroon. In East Africa sisal led the list of exports in 1913. Yet these endeavors were of only limited success. They generally meant extreme hardship for the indigenous population. The concessionary companies in Cameroon had a destructive effect on local societies, as did the plantation system in East Africa.[30]

The amount of capital invested by German companies in the African colonies during these years followed the same pattern as the government subsidies. Of 346 million marks invested, 141 million went to Southwest Africa, 106 million to East Africa, 95 million to Cameroon and 4 million to Togo.[31] Compared with the government subsidies, these figures indicate that only in Cameroon did business investment significantly exceed the cost of the colony to the German taxpayer.

In terms of overall German trade, the German colonies remained insignificant in the years before the war. Only 0.5 percent of Germany's total imports came from its colonies in 1913, while just one third of the colonies' exports went to Germany.

---

[30] Woodruff D. Smith, *The German Colonial Empire* (Chapel Hill: University of North Carolina Press, 1978), p. 85.

[31] Gann and Duignan, *The Rulers of German Africa*, p. 257. These amounts do not include the investments of individuals or mission societies.

Yet Germany's colonial trade had been increasing rapidly in the early twentieth century. British firms which had played a leading role in the commerce of Germany's West African colonies faced stiffer competition. In the prewar years Britain's percentage of Cameroon's trade declined, and by 1914 British shipping had lost the lead in the colony's commerce.[32] In German East Africa railway construction led to a lessening of dependence upon Mombasa and Zanzibar as centers for the colony's overseas trade.

In contrast to this favorable trend, Germany's position as the supplier of manufactured goods to its colonies was reduced significantly following their transfer to other colonial powers in 1919. Although tariff discrimination against foreigners did not exist in the former German colonies, other factors which tended to encourage trade between European states and their African colonies did operate there. The natural bias of a colonial administration toward businessmen of the same nationality cannot be dismissed easily. Consequently, the idea that Germany would sustain no permanent economic loss if confiscation of the German colonies was accompanied by free trade in those territories was disingenuous.

Unlike the other issues which have been discussed, German colonial war aims during the First World War did not have to be distorted by the Allies to discredit German colonialism. The German goal of widespread annexations in Africa was both real and partially public. This goal naturally influenced Western perceptions.

Given British naval superiority, the military unpreparedness of the German colonies, their lack of geographic unity and the much more powerful military potential of the Allied colonies, the Germans naturally had opposed the spread of the

---

[32] Henderson, *Studies in German Colonial History*, pp. 38 and 63. Chapter V, "British Economic Activity in the German Colonies, 1884-1914," contains a detailed discussion of the topic.

war to Africa. Once their offer of colonial neutrality had been rebuffed, their practical ability to prevent the Allied conquest of their colonies was limited.

As early as the confidential statement of German war aims contained in the September program of 1914, German Colonial Secretary Wilhelm Solf advanced far-reaching colonial claims. In the event of German victory, the Portuguese colonies, the Belgian Congo and French Equatorial Africa were to be annexed. Togo, too, was to be enlarged by the acquisition of Dahomey and part of Senegambia. For the moment nothing was demanded from Britain. In the case of Britain's defeat, however, Nigeria could be taken, thereby connecting Germany's West African acquisitions with those in central Africa.[33] The enunciated objectives of such a policy were to provide the German colonies with the geographic unity and size necessary for their defense during wartime and to provide Germany with ample supplies of raw materials in times of peace.

Henceforth, a German central African empire remained the aim of colonial enthusiasts both inside and outside the government. In a memorandum of December 26, 1916, Solf again outlined these demands, but in a more specific fashion. According to Fritz Fischer, the concept of *Mittelafrika* now was expanded to a broader vision of tropical Africa. This would allow the extension of its western boundary to include the economically developed regions of French West Africa.[34] Even in the spring of 1918, correspondence between Solf and the German Colonial Association confirmed these primary aims of colonial policy.

These goals were augmented by the German navy's hope of acquiring bases from which to threaten British shipping. With this in mind a detailed study suggested that Dakar in Senegal and Bathurst in Gambia would provide the most suitable bases.

---

[33] Fritz Fischer, *Germany's Aims in the First World War* (New York: W.W. Norton and Co., 1967), pp. 102-103.

[34] Ibid., pp. 317-318.

In addition, the study emphasized the value of acquiring islands for naval bases, including Réunion in the Indian Ocean.

Naturally, not all of these government proposals were made public. They were reflected, however, in the demands of colonial enthusiasts outside the government for extensive annexations in West and central Africa. Solf, too, made a public statement of colonial war aims following the Kreuznach Conference of 1917. Speaking to the German Colonial Society of Leipzig, Solf restricted his claims to a continuous colonial empire across central Africa.[35] Beyond the intention of appearing moderate in public, his ideas suggest the role a favorable colonial settlement might have played in a negotiated peace.

In this regard, Solf's views represented those of the minority in government. The primary aim of German wartime policy was European expansion. Fischer observes, "the colonial questions did not figure largely in the discussions of Germany's war aims; it was generally assumed that if Germany won the war they would practically realise themselves."[36]

Military Campaigns in Togo and Cameroon

Togo was the first German colony to be attacked and captured during the war. With the colony surrounded by much larger British and French possessions, the German forces there were heavily outnumbered and suffered the severe strategic

---

[35] Ibid., pp. 357-360. Meeting at Bad Kreuznach in April, a wartime council of the German government had put forward demands for widespread annexations in Europe but had referred colonial questions to the Colonial Department. For further discussion of *Mittelafrika* as a German war aim, see Hans Gatzke, *Germany's Drive to the West* (Baltimore: Johns Hopkins Press, 1950), pp. 179-181.

[36] Fischer, *Germany's Aims*, p. 590.

20

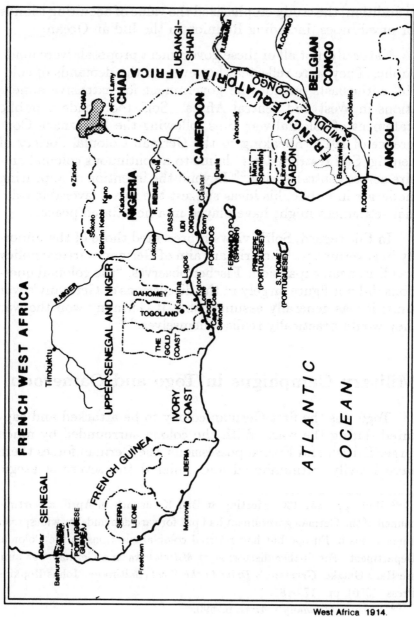

West Africa 1914.

disadvantage of having to face invading forces from all directions.[37] Before the end of August 1914, the fighting was over.

Undoubtedly realizing the difficulty of the military situation, Major von Doering, Togo's acting governor, sent messages to the Gold Coast and Dahomey proposing that neutrality be maintained between the colonies. Dispatched on August 5, the initial reply from the Gold Coast was that no response could be given until directions arrived from Great Britain. As previously noted, the instructions which were sent ordered an attack on Togo with the intention of destroying the wireless station at Kamina. Consequently on August 6, Captain F.C. Bryant, acting commander of the Gold Coast Regiment, sent two officers to Lomé to demand the surrender of the colony. Given twenty-four hours in which to reach a decision, von Doering decided to surrender the capital of Lomé and withdraw inland toward Kamina.[38]

Gold Coast forces under Bryant then advanced and occupied Lomé without opposition. Simultaneously, French colonial troops moved into eastern Togo. Bryant, assigned the temporary rank of lieutenant colonel, was placed in overall command of the Allied forces and rapidly organized an expedition to advance on Kamina. This advance proceeded along the principal German railway into the interior, with the Germans retreating before the combined Anglo-French force. Only at the village of Khra, just in front of Kamina, did the Germans make a

---

[37] F.J. Moberly, *Official History of the War: Military Operations Togoland and the Cameroons, 1914-1916* (London: His Majesty's Stationery Office, 1931), pp. 6-8. German forces have been estimated at 800 African troops and police. In addition, most of the 300 German residents in the colony had received military training. In comparison, the Gold Coast Regiment had 49 British officers and non-commissioned officers and 1,584 African troops. This was supplemented by reservists, police and volunteers numbering approximately 2,750 men. Not all of these potential British forces were needed in the conquest of Togo.

[38] Ibid., pp. 19-20.

determined stand. There, in the principal engagement of the campaign, the British and French suffered 75 casualties.[39] The Germans repulsed the Allied attack but then withdrew. Believing their military situation was now hopeless, they destroyed the wireless station at Kamina and surrendered on August 26.

A number of factors contributed to the Germans' failure to maintain a more sustained resistance in the colony. Different sources generally agree that the African population as a whole displayed little enthusiasm for the German effort. German intelligence broke down, and as a result they had difficulties in assessing the size of the advancing Allied units. Although Togo's military forces included several hundred recently mobilized Germans, many of them are reported to have had little military training. Finally, the Germans lost one of their ablest officers in an opening engagement.

Following the conclusion of the fighting, the British and French reached an agreement for the provisional partition of Togo. The British occupied the colony's western districts, including Lomé, while the French administered those in the east. This division was clearly temporary in character, but along with the leading role played by British forces in the colony's conquest, it encouraged future British claims.

In Cameroon the Allies faced a far more difficult military campaign than they had encountered in Togo. The territory's geography offered the Germans several advantages. The vast expanse of the colony provided the Germans considerable opportunity to maneuver and withdraw. Complementing this was the tropical climate of the coastal region and other areas. Dense forest meant transportation was limited to rivers, the railway network and often-rudimentary paths. This situation not only offered natural obstacles but also provided an ideal environment for ambushes and a general defensive policy of harassing an advancing enemy.

---

[39] Ibid., p. 37.

Tropical diseases, particularly malaria, created difficulties for troops in both armies. One of the British officers wrote, "Of some 3000 Europeans serving with the force, many had over a dozen malarial attacks during the eighteen months of the campaign, while scarcely any escaped altogether."[40]

Initially the Germans faced other difficulties, because of the opposition their policies had aroused among several important African leaders. Martin-Paul Samba from Ebolowa had been educated in Germany and had served as an officer in the German army. After resigning his commission in 1910, he began to plan a revolt against the Germans. This brought him into contact with Rudolph Duala Manga Bell, paramount chief of the Duala people. The Germans had alienated the Dualas by expropriating their lands.[41]

With the outbreak of the war, Samba sent a message to the French governor at Brazzaville stating his intention to revolt. The letter was intercepted by the Germans, and he was arrested along with Bell. Both men were executed on August 8, 1914.[42] As a result the Germans found themselves confronting a hostile African population at the very point where the British chose to strike.

The capture of the port of Duala was an important early British objective. It was the colony's major outlet and the terminus for Cameroon's two railway lines. At the beginning of the war it also was believed that German freighters and

---

[40] Brigadier General E. Howard Georges, *The Great War in West Africa* (London: Hutchinson and Co., 1930), p. 261.

[41] Ralph A. Austen, "Duala versus Germans in Cameroon: economic dimensions of a political conflict," *Revue française d'histoire d'Outre Mer* 64 (1977):477-497.

[42] Victor Le Vine and Roger Nye, *Historical Dictionary of Cameroon* (Metuchen, N.J.: Scarecrow Press, 1974), pp. 37 and 106-107. See also Victor Le Vine, *The Cameroons from Mandate to Independence* (Berkeley and Los Angeles: University of California Press, 1964), p. 30.

warships might have taken shelter in the good natural harbor. The operation was carried out in September 1914 by an Anglo-French force under the command of British General Charles Dobell. By sinking ships in the Cameroon Estuary, which forms the approach to Duala, and other delaying actions the Germans were able to impede the expedition's progress. Once naval action had overcome these obstacles, however, the Germans chose to withdraw from the town. They left behind considerable property, confident that the approaching German victory in Europe would allow them to return soon.[43]

Having taken Duala, Dobell realized it would be necessary to clear the area of German forces to secure the Allied position. Efforts to expand the foothold led to the conquest of the Cameroon mountain towns of Victoria and Buea. By the year's end, Allied forces also had advanced up the Northern Railway and the Wuri River and had taken Edea on the Midland Railway.

Elsewhere in Cameroon the French, assisted by the Belgians, drove up the salients into central Africa that the Germans had gained in 1911.[44] In the north, British and French forces gradually overcame all German forces except at Mora. There the German commander established himself in a nearly impregnable mountain position, which he held against repeated assaults. In the south, the Germans shifted their administrative center to Yaoundé after the loss of Duala. At Yaoundé the African population, led by Chief Karl Atangana, remained loyal to the Germans,[45] and they were able to organize the protracted defense of the colony.

---

[43] Moberly, p. 130.

[44] Ibid., p. 116.

[45] Frederick Quinn, "The impact of the First World War and its aftermath on the Beti of Cameroun," *Africa and the First World War*, ed. Melvin E. Page (New York: St. Martin's Press, 1987), p. 175.

The progress of the French and Belgian forces advancing from the east and south, under the command of General Aymerich, proved slow because of the difficult terrain and climate. In June 1915 the Germans were able to check an advance on Yaoundé by General Dobell's forces, with the Allies suffering approximately 900 casualties.[46] The rainy season, which began in July and continued through September, led to a pause in the fighting. Dobell found this a useful opportunity to send many of his forces, suffering from the severe hardships of the campaign, out of the country.

In October the Allies resumed the converging advance of their columns on Yaoundé. German resistance continued, but the Germans, outnumbered and increasingly short of ammunition, were forced to retreat into a continually contracting area. In a well-planned maneuver, the German commander, Colonel Zimmerman, abandoned Yaoundé to the Allies in January 1916 and retreated with his force of approximately 600 German and 6,000 African troops, plus an additional 8,400 non-combatants, into the Spanish territory of Rio Muni. Interned, the Germans and their African supporters, including Chief Atangana, continued to be viewed as a possible threat and were later sent out of the colony because of Allied pressure on Spain. When informed of the retreat of the main body of German troops into Rio Muni, the last German outpost (the mountain stronghold of Mora) finally surrendered in February 1916. The Allied force employed in western Cameroon under General Dobell included more than 30,000 carriers, 11,000 African troops and 1,600 Europeans. The force had been divided fairly evenly between the British and the French. About 2,500 died. General Aymerich's French and Belgian forces operating in the southern and eastern parts of the colony suffered an additional 1,800 casualties.[47]

---

[46] Henderson, p. 100.
[47] Moberly, pp. 424-427.

The character of the campaign affected Allied war aims in several ways. Given the difficult nature of the conquest, Allied military and political leaders sought territorial compensation. The rationale that the soldiers who had lost their lives in the fighting should not have died in vain supported these claims. The question of compensation also was related to the prospect of future wars and European prestige in African eyes. The British Admiralty, in particular, believed Britain had earned the right to improve its strategic position by the acquisition of Duala. Further, the British worried that their colonial position among Africans would be weakened unless their military success resulted in tangible evidence of victory.

As in Togo, the British had played a major role in the capture of Cameroon. Whether it was of greater or lesser importance than the French contribution would be a subject of controversy between the two allies. Nevertheless, if military participation was to be considered a basis for territorial reward, then the British could advance their claims. Policy makers were reluctant to acknowledge this principle in public, yet it was contemplated in the internal deliberations of both Allied governments. Finally, real or imagined insults to French troops under Dobell's command served to rekindle traditional sentiments of antagonism between the two countries.

The Arduous Conquest of East Africa

On November 12, 1918, outside of what is today the Zambian town of Kasama, a rear guard of German askaris (African troops) skirmished with pursuing soldiers of the King's African Rifles. A continent away, the western front was quiet; the First World War had come to an end the day before the last combat in Africa.

The ability of the Germans to maintain an armed force in East Africa through four years of fighting against overwhelming odds was a considerable military achievement. A number

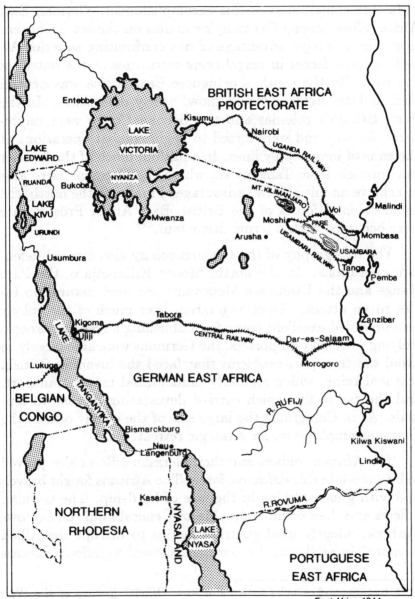

BRITISH EAST AFRICA
PROTECTORATE

Entebbe

Kisumu

Nairobi

LAKE
VICTORIA

UGANDA RAILWAY

LAKE
EDWARD

RUANDA

Bukoba

NYANZA

MT. KILIMANJARO

Voi

Malindi

LAKE
KIVU

Mwanza

Moshi

PARE

Mombasa

URUNDI

Arusha

USAMBARA RAILWAY

USAMBARA

Usumbura

Tanga

Pemba

Tabora

Zanzibar

LAKE
TANGANYIKA

Kigoma
Ujiji

CENTRAL RAILWAY

Dar-es-Salaam

Lukuga

Morogoro

GERMAN EAST AFRICA

BELGIAN
CONGO

Bismarckburg

R. RUFIJI

Neu
Langenburg

Kilwa Kiswani

Lindi

Kasama

R. ROVUMA

NORTHERN
RHODESIA

LAKE
NYASA

NYASALAND

PORTUGUESE
EAST AFRICA

East Africa 1914.

of factors contributed to this accomplishment. German East Africa, alone among Germany's colonies on the continent, enjoyed the strategic advantage of not confronting superior Allied military forces in neighboring territories at the outset of the war. To the south, Portuguese East Africa was neutral and, as later fighting would show, nearly defenseless. In the west, Britain's colonies and the Belgian Congo were unprepared for war and were forced to begin combat operations at the ends of long supply lines. In addition, much of the frontier ran through Lake Tanganyika, where the Germans were able to achieve an initial naval advantage. Finally, in the north, the small colonial forces of the British East Africa Protectorate were occupied with internal discontent.[48]

The topography of the German colony also favored defensive operations. In the north, Mount Kilimanjaro, the Pare Range and the Usambara Mountains provided natural obstacles to an attack. Thick vegetation over much of the colony also provided excellent cover for ambushing advancing troops. Relying primarily on porters, the Germans were able largely to avoid the transport problems that faced the invading British: seasonal rains, which regularly immobilized motor transport, and the tsetse fly, which carried devastating disease to animals. As in Cameroon, the large size of the colony offered the Germans ample room for strategic retreat.

The African soldiers and their German officers also proved to be a redoubtable defensive force. The Africans fought bravely and with great stamina in the face of hardship. The German officers and their commander, Major General Paul von Lettow-Vorbeck, adeptly used guerrilla tactics to disrupt the Allied advance. In addition, the Germans showed significant success

---

[48] Lieutenant-Colonel Charles Hordern, *Official History of the War: Military Operations East Africa*, Vol. 1 (London: His Majesty's Stationery Office, 1941), p. 11.

in capturing or improvising ammunition and other necessary supplies.[49]

Confronted with these obstacles the Allies – primarily the British Empire in this theater – were forced to mount a prolonged and costly offensive. The great majority of troops came from outside the British Isles, being mostly African, white South African and Indian. From London, the East African campaign almost always appeared to be of only secondary or even tertiary importance. Yet the course of the fighting was to influence concurrent and subsequent strategic thinking.

The first major engagement occurred in early November 1914, when a composite force formed primarily of Indian troops attacked the port of Tanga. Tanga was the terminus of the Northern Railway, which served the wealthy plantations of the hinterland. The British hoped to advance on both ends of the railway, enveloping and capturing the main German force in East Africa.

The assault, however, became a disaster. An overconfident and indecisive British commander with poorly prepared troops attacked the port only after von Lettow-Vorbeck had rapidly reinforced his positions. Following several days of sharp fighting, the British were obliged to withdraw to Mombasa.[50] As a result, the Germans captured a large quantity of arms and forced the British onto the defensive.

Throughout 1915 the British remained in this posture along the northern border of the German colony, which formed the principal front in East Africa. From their positions the Germans used this opportunity to send out patrols which were able to disrupt traffic on the British railway from Mombasa to Nairobi.

---

[49] Farwell, pp. 107-108, 178, 193-194 and 261-264.

[50] Charles Miller, *Battle for the Bundu: The First World War in East Africa* (New York: Macmillan Publishing Co., 1974), pp. 55-72.

The other major British military concern in the East African theater during the first year of the war was the German cruiser *Königsberg*. That this modern, fast and relatively heavily armed ship was in the western Indian Ocean at the beginning of the war was something of an accident. It had been sent to Dar es Salaam for an exhibition celebrating the completion of the Central Railway to Lake Tanganyika in the summer of 1914.[51]

With the outbreak of the war the *Königsberg* enjoyed a brief career as a commerce raider. Then, seeking a place to repair the ship's engines, the captain entered the delta of the Rufiji River south of Dar es Salaam. Eventually the British navy located the hiding place, but destroying the vessel proved more difficult.

To prevent the escape of the *Königsberg* the British were forced to guard the delta's several channels. The British could not enter the delta, however, because the deeper draft of their cruisers would cause them to run aground. At the same time the German captain, using the secondary armament from his ship, deployed a land force capable of keeping out small British patrol boats. Only the arrival of shallow-draft monitors from England finally allowed the British to enter the delta and destroy the German vessel in July 1915.[52]

During the same month, German forces on the other side of the continent, in Southwest Africa, surrendered. Despite an aborted rebellion by disgruntled Afrikaners, the South Africans had captured the Germany colony in a short and efficient campaign. In early 1916 the South African general Jan Christiaan Smuts was given command of British forces in East Africa and prepared to launch a new offensive there against the Germans.

The influx into British East Africa of a large and diverse number of troops, mainly from India and South Africa, gave

---

[51] Ibid., p. 31.

[52] Sir Julian S. Corbett, *History of the Great War: Naval Operations*, 5 vols. (London: Longmans, Green and Co., 1920-31) 3:63-67.

Smuts numerical superiority over the Germans. The British offensive, however, encountered frustrating defensive tactics which were to be repeated frequently until the end of the war. Although von Lettow-Vorbeck was pushed back, he consistently avoided encirclement. Firing from prepared positions, his troops often were able to inflict heavy casualties on the advancing columns. Finally, Smuts's soldiers suffered severely from tropical illnesses, particularly malaria and dysentery. Although these also afflicted von Lettow-Vorbeck's troops, his force was as a whole less susceptible to tropical disease. The vast majority of his troops were Africans, who were inherently more resilient to the East African environment than some of the troops from the British Empire.[53]

Still, Smuts drove down the Northern Railway toward Tanga. Then, turning off the railway, he forced von Lettow-Vorbeck back through the Nguru Mountains and on August 26, 1916, took Morogoro on the Central Railway. Dar es Salaam, too, fell to the British, and by the time torrential rains halted operations in September, the German troops were being forced south toward the Rufiji.[54] The British had captured the northern half of the colony, by far its most developed and productive part, but von Lettow-Vorbeck's forces remained intact.

The British drive had been supported by troops from the Belgian Congo, who occupied the territories of Ruanda and Urundi in the northwestern section of German East Africa. They had encountered only a skeleton force, most of the German troops having already been withdrawn. The principal Belgian difficulties were with logistics and the terrain.[55]

---

[53] Obtaining medical supplies did create problems for the Germans. Quinine was essential for fighting malaria, but the colony's normal overseas supply was cut off by the British blockade. The Germans still managed to acquire some from abroad, while German chemists in East Africa produced locally half of the wartime supplies. Henderson, p. 91.

[54] Hordern, pp. 391-393.

[55] Louis, *Ruanda-Urundi: 1884-1919*, p. 219.

After the campaign in the northern part of the colony, the composition of the British forces began increasingly to resemble that of their opponent. At the beginning of the war, the prospect of the large-scale use of black troops by the British Empire aroused dissension. Particularly in the Union of South Africa, this manifested itself in the paradoxical attitude of viewing black Africans as incapable of fighting in modern wars while at the same time fearing the future ramifications of military training for a large number of Africans.[56]

During the fighting Smuts recognized the military abilities of African troops and expressed this appreciation in letters home to South Africa. In May 1916, he wrote to the South African politician J.X. Merriman that "von Lettow has not only organized a very large Askari army but he is making them fight with great skill and bravery. They are what our Zulus or Basutos would be if properly trained." In October, he lamented to Merriman:

> Really this is not a country into which to bring a force of white men, and I have often had reason to remember your advice to send here 10,000 Zulus rather than white South Africans. The enemy of course fights with a Native army under a very limited number of white officers and is consequently not affected by tropical diseases to anything like the same degree as ourselves.[57]

---

[56] The racist attitudes of the South African government in 1915 are exemplified by the distinction which the governor general drew between recruiting "colored" and black troops. Although a battalion might be raised among the former, the latter he insisted were "less intelligent" and thus unsuitable. Harcourt Papers, 509:150.

[57] Jan Christiaan Smuts, *Selections from the Smuts Papers*, 4 vols., ed. W.K. Hancock and Jean van der Poel, (Cambridge: Cambridge University Press, 1966), 3:366 and 409.

As fighting moved into the undeveloped, tropical southern part of German East Africa, changes were made. Carriers replaced other forms of transport. By late 1917, most Indian and South African troops had been replaced with African soldiers.

In a sense, these changes heightened the cruel irony of the fighting in Africa. Von Lettow-Vorbeck believed that by continuing the campaign he was tying down British troops which might have been used in more decisive theaters of the war. With the British now relying on Africans recruited specifically to defeat von Lettow-Vorbeck, this reasoning lost its validity. More than ever, the last year of the war in East Africa saw African soldiers, under European officers, killing each other in a campaign which could have no effect on the war's general outcome.

Smuts, however, had left his East African command in January 1917, to represent the South African government at the imperial conference in London. He was to remain there as a member of the Imperial War Cabinet and later to serve as one of South Africa's representatives in the British delegation to the peace conference. Smuts was widely respected, and his voice carried particular weight in colonial questions.

Yet with regard to the campaign in East Africa, Smuts had offered the inaccurate view that it was nearly over at the end of 1916.[58] Instead, von Lettow-Vorbeck continued his stubborn resistance even as he retreated further south. He remained determined to keep an army in the field as long as possible.[59] By November 1917 the German colony's southern border, the Rovuma River, was at his back, and superior British forces were closing in upon his positions. Yet south of the river lay Portuguese East Africa, and Portugal was already at war with

---

[58] Smuts to H.J. Wolstenholme, Morogoro [East Africa], November 17, 1916, ibid., p. 411.

[59] General Paul von Lettow-Vorbeck, *My Reminiscences of East Africa* (London: Hurst and Blackett, Ltd., 1920), p. 216.

Germany. Von Lettow-Vorbeck therefore ordered most of his forces to surrender and departed south with rapidly moving columns.

The Portuguese provided little resistance. Their administration was generally unpopular and their colonial troops of poor quality. The Germans were able to capture sufficient arms and supplies to continue fighting. On several occasions British forces came close to apprehending the German columns. Yet each time the elusive von Lettow-Vorbeck slipped away. Finally, on September 28, 1918, the German troops reentered German East Africa. Von Lettow-Vorbeck then turned west into the British colony of Northern Rhodesia, where he finally surrendered after learning of the armistice in Europe.

The death and destruction caused by the fighting in East Africa far outweighed that in any of the other African theaters. Although von Lettow-Vorbeck's force may never have included more than 15,000 troops, the British are estimated to have deployed at least 160,000 soldiers against them during the length of the campaign.[60] In East and central Africa, British figures indicate that they recruited more than 50,000 African soldiers and more than one million African carriers and laborers during the fighting. Ten thousand of the Africans serving in these British military units died, while more than 100,000 of the carriers and laborers are estimated to have lost their lives during the war.[61]

The British recruited carriers from all of their neighboring colonies but drew more from German East Africa than any

---

[60] A. Adu Boahen, ed., *Unesco General History of Africa: Africa under Colonial Domination 1880-1935*, (Berkeley and Los Angeles: University of California Press, 1985), 7:291.

[61] G.W.T. Hodges, "African Manpower Statistics for the British Forces in East Africa, 1914-1918," *Journal of African History*, 19 (1978):114-115.

other area.[62] In some cases, such as with the Haya people of northwestern Tanganyika, British actions contrasted with German policy. The Germans had restricted their demands on the Haya to service in their own area. During the war, the British forced the Haya to serve far from their homes.[63]

Much of the British recruitment was forced. In the Kenyan town of Malindi, the British district commissioner reported that a call for voluntary labor in 1915 had resulted in only three responses. Relying on martial law, the government then raided the town and collected 200 laborers. In the Kisii district near Lake Victoria, people remembered years later how young men had been tricked into the service. Called into the administrative station to cut grass, they had been enrolled as porters. In August 1915 the government issued the Native Followers' Recruitment Ordinance, which authorized the conscription of Africans in Kenya for the carrier corps.[64] Wartime colonial rule did indeed bring onerous new burdens for Africans, not from one European power but from all.

[62] Ibid.

[63] Ralph A. Austen, *Northwest Tanzania under German and British Rule* (New Haven: Yale University Press, 1968), p. 125.

[64] Donald C. Savage and J. Forbes Munro, "Carrier Corps Recruitment in the British East Africa Protectorate 1914-1918," *Journal of African History*, 7 (1966):316-320.

2

West Africa:
French Expansion and British
Concessions

French Colonial Policy and
the Wartime Perspective

By the early twentieth century, the French possessions in
West and central Africa were divided into two giant colonial
federations. French West Africa reached east from Senegal to
Lake Chad, while French Equatorial Africa rose to meet it
from the banks of the Congo and the coast of Gabon. The
individual colonies in both federations had been placed under
the authority of governors general, and on a map they gave the
impression of a vast, united French empire.

From the viewpoint of French colonial enthusiasts, however, the situation was not entirely satisfactory. France had
succeeded in appropriating the great bulk of the African hinterland in the area, but along the coast French possessions
were separated by British and German colonies. Prewar Anglo-
French discussions of colonial exchanges in West Africa proved
futile.[1] Negotiators seeking arrangements favorable to their
own national interests had tended to demand greater territorial

---

[1] John D. Hargreaves, "British and French Imperialism in West Africa,
1885-1898," in *France and Britain in Africa: Imperial Rivalry and Colonial Rule*, ed. Prosser Gifford and William Roger Louis (New Haven: Yale
University Press, 1971), p. 264.

concessions than they were willing to offer. Despite these difficulties, French hope for a comprehensive settlement that would unify their West African coastal possessions and improve their access to the interior persisted in some quarters at the time of the war.

In French Equatorial Africa the basic territorial question at the outbreak of the war remained the concessions made to Germany in 1911. The French cession to Germany of the two strips along the Lobaye and Sangha rivers in central Africa virtually split the federation of French Equatorial Africa into several parts. Checked in their drive toward geographic unity, French imperialists had been furious when the territorial loss was announced.[2] The resentment endured.

Connected with efforts to consolidate the French African empire were railway plans. Colonialists saw construction from ports into the interior as the most feasible means of bringing about the economic exploitation and development of the continent. Linking these lines with each other and eventually with the Mediterranean would aid French economic penetration and military occupation of the area. The most ambitious of these projects failed because of physical difficulties and insufficient capital. Yet these dreams, too, persisted.[3]

Within the French government the Colonial Ministry was naturally a central force for colonial expansion. Officials there formulated colonial policy in conjunction with decision makers at the Foreign Ministry. Support for their activities came from those interest groups which composed the French colonial

---

[2] James J. Cooke, *New French Imperialism 1880-1910: The Third Republic and Colonial Expansion* (Hamden, Conn.: Archon Books, 1973), p. 162.

[3] Catherine Coquery-Vidrovitch, "French Colonization in Africa to 1920: Administration and Economic Development," *Colonialism in Africa 1870-1960*, 5 vols., ed. L.H. Gann and Peter Duignan (Cambridge: Cambridge University Press, 1969), 1:181.

lobby or *parti colonial.*[4] In the French legislature this body consisted of the colonial enthusiasts loosely organized as the *groupe colonial.* Outside of government, it was formed by a long list of organizations committed to French imperialism. The most significant of these with regard to Africa were the *Comité de l'Afrique française* and the *Société de Géographie.* At the time of the war, they still contained determined proponents of French colonial expansion in tropical Africa, led by men such as Auguste Terrier.[5]

Between the government officials and the colonial lobby a symbiotic relationship existed. Lobby supporters were well placed in the Colonial Ministry, and government officials regularly attended colonialist congresses. Through these opportunities and other means of access, the more important groups were able to exercise an influence on the development of policy. In turn, the propaganda of colonialist groups often generated support for colonial expansion, while they served as interest groups on whose behalf the officials could claim to be acting.

In the years just before the war general interest in French colonialism seems to have weakened. To many the occupation of Morocco in 1912 seemed a logical conclusion to expansion, and even the imperialist-minded were increasingly concerned about the prospect of war with Germany.[6] Nevertheless, at the outbreak of the war the French government still contained important voices in favor of colonial expansion in Africa. Two men who would be leading advocates of such a policy during the war were Albert Duchêne, who would become the chief of

---

[4] Stuart Persell, *The French Colonial Lobby, 1889-1938* (Stanford: Hoover Institution Press, 1983), p. 3 and C.M. Andrew and A.S. Kanya-Forstner, *The Climax of French Imperial Expansion, 1914-1924* (Stanford: Stanford University Press, 1981), pp. 23-32.

[5] Peter Grupp, "Le 'parti colonial' français pendant la première guerre mondiale. Deux tentatives de programme commun," *Cahiers d'études Africaines* 54, 14 (1974):377.

[6] Cooke, p. 165.

the African department at the Colonial Ministry in November 1918, and Emmanuel de Peretti della Rocca, head of the Foreign Ministry's African department. Both would be elected to the *Comité de l'Afrique française* shortly after the war.[7]

Above these men, Gaston Doumergue stood as the most powerful French wartime figure concerned with the annexation of Germany's African colonies. Born in the department of Gard in 1863, he had spent two years during the 1890s as an administrator in French Indochina. Later, he was elected first as a deputy and then as a senator from the Gard.[8] In Paris, he gained a reputation as both a forceful imperialist and an important politician. Indeed, he served briefly as premier in 1913, and in 1924 he would be elected president. At the outbreak of the war, he was briefly appointed foreign minister. A cabinet reshuffle in August 1914 led to his transfer to the position of colonial minister, an office he held until May 1917.

The First World War focused French eyes upon European objectives. With great unity and emotion, the French people desired the recovery of Alsace-Lorraine. Enunciated in 1914 – and the idea certainly had existed in many French minds since 1871 – this aim was maintained continuously throughout the war. As the cost of the war in lives and destruction mounted, the French leadership augmented this aim with demands for economic compensation and protection against a resurgent Germany of the future.[9] As in other European countries, the wartime French governments portrayed the conflict to the French people as a patriotic war of national defense. Nevertheless, after the initial enthusiasm for fighting dissipated,

---

[7] Andrew and Kanya-Forstner, *The Climax of French Imperial Expansion, 1914-1924*, p. 169.

[8] Roman D'Amat et R. Limouzin-Lamothe, *Dictionnaire de biographie française*, Vol. 11 (Paris: Librairie Letouzey et Ané, 1967), p. 687.

[9] David Stevenson, *French War Aims against Germany 1914-1919* (Oxford: Clarendon Press, 1982), p. 118.

French governments found themselves in the position of demanding continuing sacrifices from an increasingly war-weary public.

By the last years of the war, the horrible losses from futile trench warfare and the anti-annexationist propaganda of the socialists had contributed to growing public sentiment for morally defensible objectives. Under these circumstances the proclamation of widespread imperialist aims in Africa was likely to be unpopular with large numbers of people, particularly those on the left.[10] The reticence of government officials concerning their aims can be traced in large measure to these public attitudes.

Nor was West Africa the only area where French colonialists hoped for territorial expansion during the war. In the Middle East, the Ottoman possessions of Syria and Lebanon were particularly coveted by French imperialist circles. Some of those who thought the Levant offered the most profitable sphere for French expansion believed new acquisitions in Africa would only misdirect French energies.[11] Thus not only were colonial war aims secondary to European concerns, but their focus also was divided.

Partition Arrangements and the Development of French Colonial Designs

The conquest of the German colonies in West Africa made the establishment of some form of provisional Allied administration in them necessary. In the case of Togo this was not a complicated issue. The rapid occupation of the colony was followed by its extemporaneous partition. This was negotiated

---

[10] André Kaspi, "French War Aims in Africa, 1914-1919," in *France and Britain in Africa*, ed. Gifford and Louis, p. 378.

[11] Andrew and Kanya-Forstner, *The Climax of French Imperial Expansion, 1914-1924*, pp. 58 and 65-77.

by local French and British officials and corresponded with the areas their troops had occupied.

Cameroon presented a more difficult problem. The colony's large size and its considerable economic and strategic value stimulated conflicting French and British imperialist impulses. As the war progressed, it appeared that Cameroon represented France's best opportunity for African colonial compensation in the event of a division of Germany's colonies. Consequently, French colonialists were determined to gain as much as possible in negotiations over the colony.

With the British playing an active role in the conquest of Cameroon, an early partition agreement threatened to give them important areas which were occupied by their troops. To avoid such a contingency, French officials initially favored the administration of the colony under a condominium. During the military campaign, a joint Anglo-French administration under General Dobell theoretically existed at Duala. However, the British clearly dominated the arrangement and, as Lovett Elango shows, the Colonial Office was averse to surrendering British prerogatives.[12]

What the French therefore desired was a more equitable distribution of authority within the condominium framework. An example of the reasoning behind this approach is found in a detailed report from Governor General M.H. Merlin of French Equatorial Africa to the colonial minister, dated October 6, 1915. Writing from Brazzaville, Merlin offered his observations after paying a short visit to Duala. He noted that partition appeared to be simpler than a condominium, but he warned against it. He cautioned that despite the most prudent diplomatic reservations any partition, albeit provisional, would prejudge the future.

---

[12] Lovett Elango, "The Anglo-French 'Condominium' in Cameroon, 1914-1916: The Myth and the Reality" *International Journal of African Historical Studies*, 18, 4, (1985):670.

    To accept provisionally a division, in reality, is to tacitly admit the principle of a definitive division. At the time of the final settlement of the question, the interested party will not fail to invoke the existing condition and to establish a precedent against which it will be difficult to resist.[13]

Merlin also gave detailed suggestions as to how the government of the condominium could be established. He recommended the division of administrative functions, claiming for France the valuable public works service. This department was to include control of both the railways and public property.

There were certain parts of the German colony, however, which Merlin exempted from his proposal. These were the territories Germany had acquired from France in 1911. "Legally, the declaration of war by Germany on France had the effect of rendering the Treaty of 1911 null, as with all the other political treaties between the two powers." Furthermore, since France had reconquered all these territories since the fighting began, he reasoned that they should be returned to France on the principle of "simple restitution." To persuade Paris of this view, he provided the following analogy: "We have therefore serious claims, both in law and in fact, to demand that these territories be considered like the province of Alsace-Lorraine."[14]

These arguments appealed to Doumergue and other French imperialists. The return of the Sangha and Lobaye corridors was regarded as a foregone conclusion in case of an Allied victory. For the remainder of the colony, the merits of the condominium system seemed convincing. This proposal, however, encountered determined British opposition.

---

[13] "Possessions allemandes d'Afrique I, dossier général, avril 1914-juillet 1916," 1544:162, La Série Guerre 1914-1918, AMAE,F.

[14] Ibid., 1544:164.

Faced with an unyielding British position, the French colonialists were forced to contemplate partition. Yet if they were obliged to accept such a settlement, the French were determined to obtain the lion's share of the colony for their sphere of administration. A negotiating position along these lines was worked out on February 11, 1916, among Doumergue, de Peretti and the French diplomat Georges Picot, who was to represent France in discussions on the subject with Britain.[15]

Two days later, in a letter to Premier Aristide Briand, Doumergue provided a detailed defense of the French claims to Cameroon. His arguments deserve consideration, for they were to be repeated later as justifications for France's position. In the initial pages of the lengthy document, he recalled that France had been willing to participate in the conquest of German East Africa. Troops for this purpose had been maintained in Madagascar. That they had remained inactive was due to the decisions of British policy makers.[16]

Then, in separate sections, Doumergue formulated French pretensions to Cameroon on the basis of historic rights, military contributions, the geographic necessity of French Equatorial Africa and existing French interests in Cameroon. He recalled that French cruisers had initiated relations between France and the Cameroon coast in the 1840s. Then he developed his historic claim using a traditional device of European imperialism in Africa, treaties made with local leaders. In particular, a treaty concluded between a French naval officer and the chief of Malimba in 1883 was regarded as important because the chief's authority was said to have extended through much of the Duala area. Doumergue asserted that the chief, who reportedly was still alive, had "last year spontaneously

---

[15] Doumergue to Briand, February 13, 1916, 1044, Affaires Politiques, Archives Nationales Section Outre-Mer, Paris (AP, ANSOM) and Andrew and Kanya-Forstner, *The Climax of French Imperial Expansion, 1914-1924*, p. 97.

[16] Doumergue to Briand, February 13, 1916, pp. 3-6, 1044, AP, ANSOM.

referred to the convention of 1883 in claiming French protection."[17]

Turning to the conquest of Cameroon, Doumergue argued that the main body of the German forces always was deployed against the French colonial troops and that the total number of French soldiers employed in the campaign was greater than that of their British counterparts. The allegedly unequal treatment of the French during the campaign also seemed a valid reason for objection. For example, the French troops at Duala had been housed in the African quarter, while the British forces had claimed for themselves the better European section.

From a larger viewpoint, the geopolitical needs of French Equatorial Africa appeared to dictate French acquisition of Cameroon. The justification for this was portrayed vividly:

> If one turns one's eyes to a map of French
> Equatorial Africa, one ascertains that our colony
> has a peculiar form. A comparison often used ac-
> curately specifies that its configuration appears
> as that of a tree with its many roots represented
> by Gabon immersed in the sea, with a slim trunk
> formed by the part of the Middle Congo strangled
> between the Upper Sangha and the Oubangui and
> with vast foliage composed of the immense ter-
> ritories of Oubangui Chari Tchad. To correct
> this strange appearance, it would be necessary
> to join to it the territories that extend between
> its center and the Atlantic Ocean, which is to say
> Cameroon.[18]

---

[17] Ibid., p. 9. Even at the time these assertions were made their validity would have been questioned. Indeed the major prewar French colonialist figure, Eugène Etienne, had in 1903 admitted the worthlessness of many West African treaties because the same rights had been promised to different European states. Cooke, p. 114.

[18] Doumergue to Briand, February 13, 1916, p. 17, 1044, AP, ANSOM.

The graphic image of the French colony strangled (*"étrang-lée"*) by Cameroon provided a strong visual justification for French acquisition, which could be comprehended easily by glancing at a map of Africa. This perspective was enhanced by pointing out that completion of the German railway lines, which were extending into the interior from Duala, would make French Equatorial Africa economically dependent on Came-roon.[19]

Finally, Doumergue described France's continuing economic and commercial interests in Cameroon. He noted that the concessionary companies which had operated in the territories annexed by Germany in 1911 had continued in business. More-over, since the Allied occupation of Duala, French companies had expanded their operations there, with the encouragement of the colonial lobby in France.

The actual partition of Cameroon was not to disappoint Doumergue. After the meeting in Paris, Picot traveled to London in February 1916. Known for negotiating the more famous Sykes-Picot agreement dividing the Ottoman Empire, he also played a crucial role in diplomatic discussions over Cameroon.[20]

---

[19] Governor Merlin also recognized the strategic value of Duala and the need to secure it for France in any partition arrangement. This would have the additional benefit of foreclosing British claims on inland territories which were economically dependent on the port. See Madiba Essiben, "La France et la redistribution des territoires du Cameroun (1914-1916)," *Afrika Zamani*, 12 and 13 (December 1981), p. 50.

[20] Andrew and Kanya-Forstner, *The Climax of French Imperial Expansion, 1914-1924*, p. 99. The authors report that Picot had achieved considerable freedom in the negotiations and that this was even more remarkable because of the distinguished status of the French ambassador in London, Paul Cambon. They attribute this to Cambon's willingness to allow a subordinate to deal with the technicalities of these colonial affairs.

Picot found the British categorically opposed to the idea of a condominium.[21] The unequivocal nature of this rejection forced the French to adopt the partition alternative. Lancelot Oliphant of the British Foreign Office described the negotiating tactic which Picot adopted during their meeting of February 23:

> He emphasised once more the impatience of the Colonial Party in France at the neglect of French interests by the Quai d'Orsay and said that there was a strong desire to participate in military operations in East Africa, . . . Monsieur Picot then said that this soreness might [be] overcome and all agitation for participation in [East] Africa suppressed, if His Majesty's Government wo[uld] meet French aspirations in the Cameroons – aspirat[ions] which, he said, would necessarily be very great. On being pressed to define these desiderata, Monsieur Picot said that the port of Duala was essential and on this point there could be no compromise. He then produced a map showing that the whole of the Cameroons was desired by France with the exception of a strip along the Nigerian frontier.[22]

Yet there was to be no major colonial controversy at this point in determining the line of partition. To the surprise of the French, the British appeared ready to grant the essential territorial concessions they sought. Under these circumstances, the French were equally willing to accommodate limited British

---

[21] Grey to Cambon (draft), February 21, 1916, FO 371/2597/67347, Public Record Office, Kew, Great Britain, (PRO). Grey declared: "his Majesty's Government, after careful consideration, regret that they see the strongest objections to the proposal of the French Government that a joint régime of the nature of a condominium should be applied to the territory of the Cameroons, . . . "

[22] Oliphant memorandum, February 23, 1916, FO 371/2597, PRO.

desires. Among these the principal demands were: to unify the German section of the Emirate of Bornu with that in Nigeria; to allow the British full military use of Duala during the war; to recognize that the partition was provisional; and to acknowledge Britain's right to priority over a third power for possession of Duala, should France decide not to retain it during peace negotiations. Thus on March 3-4, 1916, the two governments agreed upon the partition of Cameroon, in an exchange of letters between French Ambassador Paul Cambon and Sir Eyre Crowe, the assistant undersecretary of state at the Foreign Office, acting in Grey's absence.[23]

A cover letter to Premier Briand from Cambon explained the provisions of the agreement and the reasons for accepting the British qualifications. He noted that the partition in the Mount Cameroon area left the French enough mountain area for a sanatorium, a purpose for which its climate was believed to be well suited. About the provisional character of the agreement he wrote, "The English vigorously insisted on the acceptance of this point of view and this can be well understood because the compensation that they will obtain in East Africa is still to be conquered, while our part is secured."[24]

Years later, Oliphant described the partition, discussing his motives and those of the British cabinet. According to this later account, he was informed by the foreign secretary that the unfavorable course of the war on the western front was having a "most depressing effect" on France and that the cabinet had resolved to grant the French all of Cameroon, "in the hope that such action would act as a stimulating tonic."[25]

---

[23] Cambon to Grey, March 3, 1916 and Crowe to Cambon, March 4, 1916, 1544, La Série Guerre 1914-1918, AMAE,F.

[24] Cambon to Briand, March 4, 1916, ibid.

[25] Sir Lancelot Oliphant, *An Ambassador in Bonds* (London: Putnam and Co., 1946), p. 34. This description is included in an autobiographical introduction to the story of his arrest and imprisonment by the Germans during the Second World War, when he was ambassador to Belgium.

Oliphant continues, "Whether owing to my ancestry, my time in oriental bazaars or sheer cussedness I can't say, but this idea did not appeal to me."[26] Instead, he won permission to offer the French only as much of Cameroon as they requested. "Now Monsieur Picot was a good patriot: but even so, it never dawned on him to ask for the *whole* of the Kamerun." Thus, "a strip of land had been saved for the Empire amounting to over 34,000 square miles..., marching with the whole eastern frontier of Nigeria. Apart from good natural products and a population of nearly a million, the territory also had an excellent potential hill-station near Bali."[27]

To the extent that the foregoing explanation can be accepted, we are provided with an illustration of the personal element in the development of colonial history. In addition, Oliphant's unrestrained desire for territorial acquisition is illustrative of an attitude characteristic of many British statesmen dealing with imperial affairs.

It is prudent, however, to accept the author's claims with some reserve. His book, written thirty years after the event, departs in places from descriptions written in 1916. Read alone, it has the potential to exaggerate the historical role of an individual, while at the same time failing to integrate the partition into its colonial context. For example, in 1946 Oliphant stated that he had agreed on the spot to Picot's proposed division. Yet in Oliphant's own memorandum of 1916, he wrote, "We confined ourselves to stating that we would submit his desiderata to our Government."[28]

A contemporary account of British thinking can be found in a letter from Foreign Secretary Grey to Lord Francis Bertie, British ambassador in Paris. In it, Grey describes his conversation with French Ambassador Cambon and explains the

---

[26] Ibid.

[27] Ibid., p. 35.

[28] Oliphant memorandum, February 23, 1916, FO 371/2597, PRO.

reasons for the British government's decision largely to accept the French proposals for Cameroon. Grey had told Cambon that British "Colonial feeling was equally excited about Duala," but he acknowledged to Bertie that "Duala was the only possible port for French Central Africa."

Perhaps more important, Cambon had stated that if the French received Duala, "they should drop their demands about German East Africa." Grey acknowledged, too, that the occupation of German Southwest Africa by the Union of South Africa provided a further basis for the traditional policy of colonial compensation, with the British acquiescing to French demands for Cameroon in exchange for a free hand elsewhere.[29]

This description accurately reflects the conclusions reached by the War Committee on February 22. The minutes of the meeting suggest, however, that differences of opinion existed and that the question was considered in some detail. Grey, agreeing that "there was a good deal in the French claim," had raised justifications based both on the suffering of France and on imperial gains made by Britain as a result of the war. Andrew Bonar Law, the current colonial secretary, was willing to accept this position in exchange for a French *quid pro quo* that they would not raise claims in East Africa. Not unexpectedly, the first lord of the admiralty, Arthur James Balfour, and Admiral Sir Henry Jackson made the strongest arguments concerning Duala's strategic importance.

David Lloyd George then urged that the British "ought to deal generously with the French" and suggested that the question be considered from the French perspective in the event of a compromise peace. Grey took up this line of reasoning and surmised that the French might then say, "We may still have the Germans on our territory in the North of France, but on the other hand we are running the German colony of the

---

[29] Grey to Bertie, draft, February 24, 1916, FO 371/2597, PRO.

Kameruns."[30] In spite of this approach, the fundamental focus of the meeting remained on using concessions in Cameroon as compensation for other British colonial gains.

As one might expect, the reaction in Paris was one of delight. Auguste Terrier, who in the spring of 1916 was leading a newly formed subcommission of the *Société de Géographie* studying African questions with regard to a future peace settlement, responded that the agreement "is very advantageous and even surpasses the hopes of the French colonialists."[31] In addition to the division of the German colonies, his subcommission also considered the possibility of a territorial redistribution of Africa and a revision of the international acts which restricted French authority on the continent. Terrier focused much of his work on the unification of French West Africa. To accomplish this he argued that France should acquire Gambia, Sierra Leone, the Gold Coast and Togo, along with an adjustment of the border between Nigeria and Chad.[32]

Still at the Colonial Ministry, Doumergue offered an illuminating view of French aims in Africa, and particularly Cameroon, during the fall of 1916. His ideas, consistent with those he had earlier expressed to Briand, are recorded in a letter from the Belgian minister in Paris, Baron Edmond de Gaiffier d'Hestroy, to the Belgian premier, Baron Napoléon Eugène Beyens. Dated October 12, 1916, and marked "Very Confidential," the letter reports on a revealing conversation held at the end of the preceding week between de Gaiffier and Doumergue.

---

[30] Minutes of the Seventy-Third Meeting of the War Committee, February 22, 1916, CAB 22/8/66502, PRO.

[31] Grupp, pp. 380-381.

[32] Ibid., p. 381 and C.M. Andrew and A.S. Kanya-Forstner, "The French Colonial Party and French Colonial War Aims, 1914-1918," *Historical Journal*, 17 (1974):89.

Doumergue is portrayed as determined to retain Cameroon, as he allegedly argues:

> French Equatorial Africa was necessarily handicapped by the Treaty of November 4, 1911, the two German expropriations on the Congo and the Ubangui rendering unexploitable the eastern part of the colony. We have repaired the committed error, and more, we administer Cameroon, which we occupied militarily, and we will keep it.[33]

Continuing, Doumergue expressed support for the trans-Saharan railway. He suggested the role it might play in economic development and stated the French intention to continue the German railway construction from Duala toward French Equatorial Africa and the Belgian Congo.

De Gaiffier's account closes with another of Doumergue's image-provoking assessments: "Your colony suffers from an insufficient access to the Ocean.... We suffer from the same problem as you: our window on the Ocean does not open widely enough."[34]

Efforts to Define French Aims: 1917-18

Events in the spring and summer of 1917 did not seem to portend an Allied victory. Russia was on the verge of military collapse and slipping into revolutionary chaos. On the western front the ill-conceived Nivelle offensive proved a disaster. Among the French troops the enormous and seemingly pointless losses had led to rampant disaffection and actual mutiny in some units. When General Philippe Pétain assumed command in May 1917, he endeavored to restore order and morale and realized it would be necessary to remain on the defensive until the arrival of American forces.

---

[33] De Gaiffier to Beyens, October 12, 1916, Af 1/2, AMAE,B.
[34] Ibid.

Military setbacks were accompanied by political instability in France. Briand was forced to resign in March, and the short Ribot and Painlevé ministries followed. Finally, on November 16, Georges Clemenceau became premier. Determined to fight on until the elusive victory was achieved, he also assumed the Ministry of War and governed in a semidictatorial fashion.

As these events unfolded, French colonialists sought to increase public support for their designs by emphasizing the military and economic contributions of the colonies to the war effort. France's African colonies were portrayed as an almost-inexhaustible source of soldiers to a nation bled dry by a war of attrition. In 1910, then Lieutenant Colonel Charles Mangin, concerned by France's falling birthrate, had proposed this idea in his book, *La force noire*. He wrote that in a prolonged European conflict, "our African Forces would constitute almost indefinite reserves." Mangin praised their fighting qualities and predicted that "their arrival on the battlefield would produce a considerable moral effect on the adversary."[35]

In practice, the use of African troops in Europe proved much less successful than such grandiloquent claims. During the Nivelle offensive they sustained heavy losses.[36] It became widely accepted among the French military that they were unable to endure Europe's cold winters. The recruitment drives in West Africa produced more moderate numbers than the French rhetoric promised.

Shortly before the war, the African Blaise Diagne had been elected to the French Chamber of Deputies from Senegal. He worked to strengthen the rights of Senegalese to French citizenship, accepting in turn the obligation of military service. By

---

[35] Lieutenant-Colonel Charles Mangin, *La force noire*, troisième édition (Paris: Librairie Hachette, 1911), p. 343.

[36] Marc Michel, *L'Appel à l'Afrique: Contributions et réactions à l'effort de guerre en A.O.F. 1914-1919* (Paris: Publications de la Sorbonne, 1982), pp. 318-321.

November 1917, 90,000 soldiers had been recruited in French West Africa. The following year Diagne was appointed commissioner of the republic and charged with responsibility for a new recruitment drive in West Africa. In French West and Equatorial Africa at least another 72,000 troops were recruited, although the end of the war that year meant most never reached the front.[37] Many Africans criticized Diagne's involvement.

The French governments argued that the African troops were volunteers, but this was true of only a fraction of the men. With regard to the West African recruiting campaign of 1915-16, Marc Michel writes: "Of the 52 or 53,000 men recruited, only 7,000 (13.4 or 13.2%) were volunteers 'in the real sense of the word' according to Clozel [the governor general] himself."[38] Africans often would flee or even mutilate themselves to avoid what was in reality conscription. Finally, in many places, there were actual revolts.[39]

In this uncertain environment, the French government finally began the process of systematically analyzing its wartime colonial objectives. On October 5, 1917, the colonial minister issued instructions for the creation of a commission charged with organizing and classifying information on colonial aims.[40] Entitled the *Commission de documentation coloniale*, the new body held its first meeting on October 26. André You, chief of the African department in the Colonial Ministry, was named president of the commission.

---

[37] C.M. Andrew and A.S. Kanya-Forstner, "France, Africa and the First World War," *Journal of African History* 19 (1978):14-17.

[38] Michel, p. 84.

[39] M. Crowder, "The 1914-1918 European War and West Africa," *History of West Africa*, 2 vols., ed. J.F.A. Ajayi and M. Crowder (London: Longman Group, 1974), 2:498-500.

[40] Minutes of the meeting of October 26, 1917, *Commission de documentation coloniale*, 3254 6, AP, ANSOM.

Albert Duchêne, who would follow You as head of the African department in November 1918, quickly emerged as a preponderant force in policy development. Duchêne focused his energies on issues relating to Africa. At the initial meeting, Duchêne argued vigorously for an assertion of the Colonial Ministry's preeminence in colonial policy formulation. "To this Ministry," he declared, "belongs the direction of France's colonial policy."[41]

The commission approached colonial topics by posing questions and then responding to them with reports and discussion. The contemplation of general matters related to Africa opened with a question of the broadest nature. To what extent was it possible to extend the block of France's West and central African possessions?[42] The commissioners focused their discussion on the territories in the vicinity of their colonies, but they also chose to muse over the old dream of connecting their colony on the Somali coast with their possessions in West Africa.

The idea of France's African empire sweeping in an unbroken expanse from the Atlantic to the Indian Ocean is an arresting thought in the midst of the First World War. Raised only as a speculative contingency, it still suggests the wide limits of colonial rearrangement that the commission was willing to consider. Of course, it was not a new idea. It had emerged in the ambitions of some French colonialists in the 1880s and 1890s. Yet the Fashoda affair of 1898 appeared to have dashed French hopes. To accomplish the project in 1917, France still needed to acquire the Sudan and much of Ethiopia. The first of these was jealously regarded by Britain as basic to its position in Egypt, and the latter was coveted by Italy.

Given France's wartime alliances with Britain and Italy, the African territory could not have been gained as a result of conquest, and even raising the question with the Allies would

---

[41] Ibid.

[42] Minutes of the meeting of November 16, 1917, ibid.

have been likely to provoke rancor and mistrust. This almost-foregone conclusion was delivered on December 7 by You. He observed "that all were in agreement on the futility of pursuing a territorial extension toward the east, which is moreover impossible and dangerous, as M. Duchêne has very well demonstrated."[43]

In West Africa actual adjustments of colonial frontiers received more serious consideration. It was recognized that the British were never likely to give up Nigeria. Yet, the prospects of acquiring other colonies along the West African coast were more hopefully envisioned. With regard to a question about border alterations with Gambia, Portuguese Guinea, Sierra Leone, Liberia and Togo, Duchêne argued on February 1, 1918, that "we clearly must strive for the total disappearance of these troublesome enclaves."[44]

If these large changes were not possible, however, Duchêne did not in general support simple boundary adjustments, which he thought would prove costly. Only in the case of Togo was he willing to modify this attitude. There he argued that one could usefully envision a border alteration with Dahomey. Since Togo was a German colony under French occupation, the change was not likely to be expensive.

Approaching the topic from a different direction, the commission's president raised concerns about what might be offered in colonial exchanges. Speaking of Dahomey, he recalled its value in terms similar to those used to describe French interests in Cameroon. He remarked that "if the Territory of Dahomey escaped from our sovereignty, it would be at the same time the closing of an outlet on the sea and that as a result we would become tributaries of foreign possessions like that of the British railway from Kano."[45]

---

[43] Minutes of the meeting of December 7, 1917, ibid.

[44] Minutes of the meeting of February 1, 1918, ibid.

[45] Minutes of the meeting of January 25, 1918, ibid.

Among these more general African issues, the disposition of Cameroon was of pivotal importance. Even in the initial discussions its importance to French Equatorial Africa was emphasized. Illustrative of this was Duchêne's unambiguous statement on November 16, 1917: "On the conservation of Cameroon depends the future of our Equatorial Africa. We must seek to secure it for ourselves at any price."[46]

Detailed arguments in favor of the above position were developed by the Colonial Ministry's African section. The product of these labors was a report which Duchêne presented to the commission on March 8, 1918. As might have been anticipated, the meeting adopted the report's conclusions.

In twenty-seven pages of disputation, all the grounds for French retention of the German colony were reviewed. The report described the development of French claims during the war and made ample use of Doumergue's earlier reasoning in favor of them, relying heavily on his letter of February 13, 1916. Historic, geographic and economic arguments were expounded. Behind these arguments stood the underlying motive of the relationship of Cameroon to France's existing colonies. "Thus the question of Cameroon must be considered less from the angle of the intrinsic value of the conquered territories, than from that of their usefulness with regard to the future of Equatorial Africa."[47]

The report also raised the question of the future treatment of the African inhabitants of Cameroon by the Germans, should the colony be returned to them. Noting the attachment the Africans had shown to the Allies, unfavorable consequences for them were foreseen: "Placing the natives of Cameroon again under the German yoke, already extremely harsh before

---

[46] Minutes of the meeting of November 16, 1917, ibid.

[47] "Modifications territoriales à prevoir à l'issue de la guerre; Questions propres à l'Afrique Equatoriale et Centrale," No. 22, p. 9, 3254 6, AP, ANSOM.

the war, would without doubt have as a consequence measures of severe reprisal."[48] The voicing of this humanitarian issue is representative of explanations increasingly used in public toward the end of the war to justify the confiscation of Germany's colonies.

Another new topic which the commission confronted was the growing sentiment in certain Allied circles for some form of international regime which would exercise authority in the former German colonies and possibly over other areas of tropical Africa. Again the propelling motive appeared to be humanitarian in nature, seeking both to remove Africans from European conflicts and to prevent European rivalries over African possessions.

The concept, however, encountered a hostile atmosphere among the commission's members. On January 11, 1918, Duchêne called for the outright rejection of any idea proposing the internationalization of colonies in Africa. Addressing a meeting of the commission, he argued that the resulting supranational regime would lead to constant quarreling and eventually impotence. Any real African self-determination, through such means as plebiscites, he likewise denounced as impractical.[49] Discussion at the meeting echoed his sentiments.[50]

Instead proposals compatible with the French doctrine of assimilation were put forward.[51] These suggested that guarantees of natural rights, individual liberties, the exercise of jus-

---

[48] Ibid., p. 25.

[49] "Modifications territoriales à prevoir à l'issue de la guerre; Questions générales," No. 5, p. 12, ibid.

[50] Minutes of the meeting of January 11, 1918, ibid.

[51] Assimilation, which maintained that French colonial subjects should absorb French culture and aspire to French rights, had been challenged by the idea of association. Under the system of association African leaders were employed as administrative agents, while it was expected that the indigenous population would retain its traditional culture. Nevertheless, French officials believed the protection of individual liberty which charac-

tice and other promises might be made. Should such pledges be offered in general, France would have no reason to object, provided of course that each power remained the sole judge of measures in its territories.[52]

Even while the *Commission de documentation* was continuing its deliberations, a further impetus was given to the development of colonial war aims. In February 1918 a new commission, *La Commission d'étude des questions coloniales posées par la guerre*, was created. An inter-ministry commission, its membership included individuals of considerable political prominence: Léon Bourgeois, Théophile Delcassé, Gaston Doumergue and Eugène Etienne as well as civil servants and politicians.[53] The colonial minister, Henri Simon, was appointed president.

At the first meeting, on February 11, 1918, the purpose of the new commission was defined. Simon pointed out the existence of the earlier commission and described its work as the documentary study of colonial questions. This was not to be the role of the new group. "You are not, in fact, an administrative commission charged with examining details, with collecting and deciding on documentation," he told them. Rather the new body was a "political commission" whose membership qualified it to develop solutions to problems at the end of the war.[54] The background of the colonial enthusiasts on the commission also predisposed it toward colonial expansion.

Simon acknowledged a certain embarrassment at chairing such a distinguished body. He also anticipated that he would be unable to attend most of the commission's meetings and

terized Republican France was reflected in the nation's colonial policies.

[52] Minutes of the meeting of January 11, 1918, p. 14.

[53] Andrew and Kanya-Forstner, *The Climax of French Imperial Expansion, 1914-1924*, p. 150.

[54] Minutes of the meeting of February 11, 1918, *Commission d' étude des questions coloniales posées par la guerre*, 97, AP, ANSOM.

asked its members to select two vice presidents. Bourgeois was approached, but he declined, saying he would not have sufficient time. Etienne and Doumergue then were chosen unanimously as the vice presidents.[55] Etienne once had been the leader of the French colonial party, but he was now in his seventies and less active. Thus, Doumergue again assumed a dominant role in an effort to develop colonial policy.

Presiding at the next meeting, Doumergue offered his views on what he believed were the two complementary aims of that policy. First, France had a civilizing mission in its colonial empire, the exercise of which was in the interest of humanity. Second, the colonies were necessary for the existence and development of French industry and commerce.[56]

In the economic category, the colonies acted both as sources of raw materials and as markets for French products. The value of these contributions was likely to be increased at the end of the war. The destruction caused in the departments of the north and east by the fighting would require raw materials for rebuilding. The anticipated return of Alsace-Lorraine, provinces of significant industrial production, accompanied by the likely establishment of protective tariffs, would make the colonies essential outlets for French manufacturing.

French businessmen, however, did not automatically provide the anticipated support for this line of reasoning.[57] M. Pralon, vice president of *La Commission de direction du comité des forges*, responded in an equivocal fashion to Doumergue's request that he explain the metal industry's colonial needs. Pralon noted France's shortage of coal and agreed with Doumergue that the colonies might become a source of raw materials and a market. Yet, he continued, "Until now the colonies have

---

[55] Ibid.

[56] Minutes of the meeting of February 25, 1918, ibid.

[57] Andrew and Kanya-Forstner, *The Climax of French Imperial Expansion, 1914-1924*, p. 147.

not been large markets for our industry, with several exceptions, because the French colonies have been small consumers of metal products."[58]

In this picture of limited economic value, he did acknowledge a brighter area that French colonialists might have seen as useful in their efforts to annex Togo and Cameroon. "It is especially in the form of railway material that French metallurgy has found a market in the colonies," he said.[59] It would not be surprising if the French colonial enthusiasts made a connection between this thought and their view of the German colonies as routes to their colonial hinterland.

This conception of the German colonies naturally was contained in Duchêne's presentation of the West and central African findings of the *Commission de documentation* to the *Commission d'étude*. He repeated his earlier argument that it would be "chimerical" to attempt to revive the old projects aimed at connecting French colonies in West and East Africa. Rather, France's current interest must be to "strengthen the unity" of its existing African empire. He remarked that claiming Togo and Cameroon would be a "highly legitimate" demand if the German colonies were not returned. In fact, with regard to the role that France had played in military operations both in Europe and outside of Europe, the claim was also "very moderate."[60]

The territories which had been ceded to Germany in 1911 were seen as a particular threat to the unity of France's possessions. These "two antennas" nearly had severed the connection of the territories south of Lake Chad; only the link formed by the equatorial African rivers had prevented their unity from being completely broken.

---

[58] Minutes of the meeting of April 15, 1918, 97, AP, ANSOM.

[59] Ibid.

[60] Minutes of the meeting of June 24, 1918, ibid.

The acquisition of Togo fit into the pattern of improving access to the ocean for France's possessions in the interior of West Africa. "It would permit the widening of the corridor that forms Dahomey."[61] In connection with this argument, the addition of Lomé to the French zone was seen as "very desirable" for the extension of the Dahomean littoral.

Duchêne's presentation provides a restatement of many of the significant motives behind French designs on Germany's colonies. Most important, French colonialists focused their attention on Cameroon and Togo because of their geographic value to France's African empire. In one statement of war aims after another, both colonies were portrayed as gateways to French possessions. In this respect, Cameroon's relationship with French Equatorial Africa was naturally of more importance.

Additional reasons for French colonial expansion certainly existed. Colonial enthusiasts dreamed of the economic development of the German colonies and the benefits this would bring to France. The prospect of Cameroon as a market for French products and a source of raw materials complemented its strategic value. The German colonies were seen, too, as representing compensation due France both for its military effort and for the colonial gains that Britain would make elsewhere.

Beyond these perceived benefits, there was fear of future German colonialism in Africa. This concern was conceived as in the best interests of the Africans, but its primary impetus was protecting France's empire from future encroachments.

A new threat to French colonial ambitions also was emerging by the end of the war. The source of this apprehension was the growing appeal of an impartial colonial settlement, a settlement which would be anti-imperialist. Not surprisingly, French colonialists glimpsed the possibility that such an arrangement would not necessarily conform with their ambitions. Britain

---

[61] Ibid.

was willing to reach a colonial compromise, but it was these new ideas embodied in the Wilsonian program which remained capable of disrupting French aims.

Whitehall's Policies:
Security and Accommodation

In West and central Africa two compatible motives shaped British policies. The first concern of British officials was to protect their shipping lanes and communications. This objective prompted the initial British attack on the German colonies. Later British statesmen sought to use territorial concessions in Togo and Cameroon as a means to compensate France for colonial gains they expected to make elsewhere.

Beyond these two guiding motives, other factors entered into British decision making with regard to Togo and Cameroon. Individual and departmental priorities, perceived African interests, British military participation and the colonies' economic potential all were considered at one time or another.

The Colonial Office, which administered Britain's colonies in West and East Africa, was not a large bureaucratic organization in the early twentieth century. The establishment, from the permanent undersecretary down to the second-class clerks, "the second lieutenants of administration," included fewer than fifty men in 1914. Not quite on par with the Foreign Office, it was nevertheless a respectable service. Its senior officers often had top academic honors from Oxford or Cambridge.[62] Lewis Harcourt had entered the House of Commons as a Liberal in 1904 and in 1910 became colonial secretary. More than many of his predecessors, Harcourt took an active and detailed interest in the development of Colonial Office policy.

---

[62] L.H. Gann and Peter Duignan, *The Rulers of British Africa 1870-1914* (Stanford: Stanford University Press, 1978), pp. 50-51 and 63.

By 1914, however, the formation of British imperial policies involved a larger number of participants than just those at
the Colonial Office. The Foreign Office, the Admiralty and the
Board of Trade all sought to influence wartime decisions. In
addition, Britain's self-governing Dominions were in the process of strengthening their role in British decision making on
matters which concerned them. Imperial participation in the
war effort would accelerate this development.[63]

Colonial Secretary Harcourt played a direct role in the early
conduct of the colonial campaigns. At the same time, he sought
the advice of colonial officials and officers on the disposition of
Togo and Cameroon.

A detailed memorandum from Hugh Clifford, governor of
the Gold Coast, recorded his views on "the most satisfactory
permanent settlement which can be arrived at between Great
Britain and France with regard to the future of Togoland."[64]
He acknowledged that his analysis represented only a local perspective and presented alternatives ranging from a return to
Germany to territorial exchanges with France. Yet, his report
clearly offered arguments in favor of British retention of the
colony.

Clifford saw the return of Togo to Germany as "extremely
inexpedient." Africans, he alleged, disliked German rule, frequently referring to the Germans as "25ers" for the number of
lashes they assigned.[65] In contrast, the population is described

---

[63] Nicholas Mansergh, *The Commonwealth Experience*, 2 vols., revised
edition (Toronto: University of Toronto Press, 1983), 1:191-201.

[64] Memorandum prepared by Clifford at Harcourt's request, Government House, Accra, October 1914, Harcourt Papers, 476a, BLO.

[65] Although Clifford's portrait certainly was influenced by the wartime
situation, historians often view the Germans as having relied more on corporal punishment than the British. German policy actually varied greatly,
differing between districts and changing over time. See Arthur Knoll, *Togo
Under Imperial Germany 1884-1914* , pp. 68-71.

as welcoming the British forces. He foresaw the Germans taking retribution on the Africans and suggested that the colony's restoration to Germany "would be a very serious blow to our prestige among natives" of the Gold Coast.[66] Further, Clifford described many Africans as favoring union with the Gold Coast because it would mean an end to ethnic divisions created by the existing colonial boundaries.

There is evidence that the governor's analysis did reflect the opinions of at least some articulate Africans. Even before the war, an African newspaper published at Cape Coast, the *Gold Coast Leader*, had contained a column that voiced African grievances in Togo.[67] To avoid detection by the Germans, the correspondent had used the pen name "A Native of Aneho," referring to a Togolese town.

The correspondent's articles before the war had criticized German colonial policy and their behavior toward Africans.[68] When the British occupied the colony in August 1914 the mood of the column changed to rejoicing. "Hurrah! Hurrah!! Hurrah!!! *Togoland ist English geworden* – Togoland has become English."[69] The following month he continued his praise for

---

[66] Memorandum prepared by Clifford, Harcourt Papers, 476a, BLO.

[67] A vigorous African press had existed since the nineteenth century in Britain's West African colonies. Newspaper publishing developed more slowly and on different lines in France's African territories. They lacked comparable African-owned papers during the First World War and the peace conference. See Frank Barton, *The Press of Africa: Persecution and Perseverance* (London: Macmillan Press, 1979), pp. 16-21 and 60-61. A brief description of the different African-owned and -operated newspapers in the Gold Coast can be found in K.A.B. Jones-Quartey, *A Summary History of the Ghana Press 1822-1960* (Accra: Ghana Information Services Department, 1974), pp. 17-21.

[68] A Native of Aneho, "The Germans in Togoland," *Gold Coast Leader*, see January 10, 1914, p. 5; April 18, 1914, p. 5; July 18, 1914, p. 5; and August 1, 1914, pp. 4-5.

[69] "The English in Togoland," *Gold Coast Leader*, August 29, 1914, p. 5.

British administration: "It is lawful and right that Togoland should be an English Colony. It is the wish of the natives from time immemorial that it should be so."[70]

With respect to a territorial settlement with France, Governor Clifford pointed out that an equal partition was not feasible. It was impractical to divide Lomé from the railway lines which connected it with the interior. As a result, the power which received these assets would gain most of the colony. He did argue, however, that Britain's greater military contribution gave it "a preferential claim."

Clifford also raised the possibility of Britain receiving both Togo and Dahomey from France. This would have created a united British West African bloc, leading eventually to a decline in administrative costs. However, neither of the two colonies was "intrinsically" of any significant worth. Clifford acknowledged that the French might have objected to this plan because of an intention to use Dahomey as an outlet for their African hinterland, but the extent of the conviction behind such a protest was uncertain. Dahomey's railway was incomplete, and France could be expected to "attach far greater importance to" Cameroon.[71]

Harcourt replied to Clifford that the memorandum would be "most useful to me when we come to settle these matters."[72] The report's similarity to the French aim of unifying their West African possessions is evident, although Clifford places considerably less value on this objective. It also shows a resemblance to the French predisposition at least to consider the maximum territorial goals they might hope to achieve.

With regard to Cameroon, two directions and rationales for British expansion quickly emerged. Sir Frederick Lugard,

---

[70] "The English in Togoland," *Gold Coast Leader*, September 19, 1914, p. 4.

[71] Memorandum prepared by Clifford, Harcourt Papers, 476a, BLO.

[72] Harcourt to Clifford, November 25, 1914, ibid.

the British governor of Nigeria, seized upon the war as an opportunity to recover possessions for the African rulers of Bornu and Adamawa. Their precolonial territories had been divided by the border between Nigeria and Cameroon. Both African states found some of their former dependencies located in Cameroon, and this had caused complications for African political relations.[73]

In Bornu, the Shehus of the al Kanemi dynasty had been conquered in 1893 by Rabeh Zubair from the Sudan. Rabeh established a fortified capital at Dikwa, in the eastern part of Bornu, but was himself defeated in 1900 by French forces advancing into the region. The subsequent colonial partition of the territory in the early twentieth century assigned Dikwa to the Germans while leaving the greater part of Bornu in British hands. On both sides of the border the al Kanemi dynasty was restored, and the rulers were closely related.[74]

South of Bornu, the emirate of Adamawa was governed by the lamido at the town of Yola. Before the Anglo-German partition, the lamido exercised an overlordship throughout much of western Cameroon. Not only were many of these dependencies placed under German rule, but the border delimitation exacerbated the sense of injustice felt in Yola. South of the town many of the best grazing lands were left on the German side of the border. To the north, rivers were used to form the boundary, severing villages from their farmlands. "They have left me merely the latrines of my kingdom," complained the displeased lamido.[75]

---

[73] Akinjide Osuntokun, *Nigeria in the First World War* (London: Longman Group, 1979), pp. 212-214.

[74] S.J. Hogben and A.H.M. Kirk-Greene, *The Emirates of Northern Nigeria* (London: Oxford University Press, 1966), pp. 333-342 and 350-352.

[75] A.H.M. Kirk-Greene, *Adamawa: Past and Present* (London: Oxford University Press, 1958), p. 67.

On the coast, Lugard and General Dobell, the British commander of the campaign, placed a high priority on the retention of Duala. The French had not participated in the capture of the port, and it offered an invaluable naval base. "The natural strength of Duala makes it imperative that it should never be in the hands of a possible future enemy," wrote Dobell. He supported this argument by referring to a defense paper prepared by a German naval officer in the preceding year. He concluded, "I do not consider it would ever be possible to capture the place if properly defended."[76]

Dobell's analysis was not, however, devoid of other concerns. He pointed out that "the natives here are more English than in any other part of West Africa and I am sure they would very much resent being handed over to the French."[77] He suggested a demarcation line of the Sanga River, thereby claiming for Britain the large area of northwestern Cameroon.

Again, Harcourt responded by promising to keep the general's views in mind and noted that the British were seeking Duala in a temporary partition of the colony with France. The extent of the colonial secretary's agreement with the views of his officials can be seen in a cabinet paper he prepared in 1915. Entitled "The Spoils," it provided Harcourt's colleagues with an analysis of what territories might be obtained by Britain, assuming an Allied victory.

With respect to West Africa, Harcourt discussed the difficulties of dividing Togo. One possible solution he suggested to this problem was the one just discussed: France might give up Togo and Dahomey for concessions elsewhere, and Britain then would be able to unite all its territories in the area. In Cameroon, Harcourt wrote, "We might ourselves retain very much less than one-fourth of the area, but what it is essential

---

[76] Dobell to Harcourt, Government House, Duala, October 8, 1914, Harcourt Papers, 463, BLO.

[77] Ibid.

that we should have is the northern railway (about 80 miles) from Duala to Baré; Mount Cameroon on the coast, which will make a perfect sanatorium for the whole of West Africa; and the town and harbour of Duala."[78]

The resulting provisional partition of Cameroon in 1916 did not put an end to British discussions of the colony's role in a future peace settlement. Later that year, the topic was reviewed by the subcommittee on territorial changes of the Committee of Imperial Defence. Headed by Sir Louis Mallet, this interdepartmental subcommittee had been established by an order of the prime minister on August 27. It was charged with considering territorial changes which might occur in Africa and other areas outside of Europe as a consequence of the war. The subcommittee's proposals on Cameroon and Togo generally conformed with the political decisions reached earlier. Yet a survey of the subcommittee's materials reveals a divergence over strategy, reflecting the particular interests of different government departments.

Placing the German colonies into the general question of postwar strategy led to a clash between two British foreign policy traditions: the balance of power in Europe and naval supremacy. The first of these policies was argued in a general staff memorandum which supported the maintenance of a strong Germany in central Europe. "Such a State must possess some outlet for its surplus population, and some area from whence to draw those raw materials which are only procurable in the tropics."[79]

The memorandum asserted that Germany's lost colonies would become a new Alsace-Lorraine, making permanent peace

---

[78] Harcourt memorandum, "The Spoils," March 25, 1915, CAB 37/126/27, PRO.

[79] "Note by the General Staff as to the Policy to be Pursued in Regard to the German Colonies," T.C. 4, September 8, 1916, CAB 16/36/66737, PRO.

impossible. Under such circumstances the German surplus population would move toward the Americas where, as events in the war had demonstrated, German influence could have negative consequences for Britain's interests. Finally, it raised the concern that unless Germany was completely defeated it might seek a restoration of its colonies, and then the Allies would have to consider "whether it is worth while to expend thousands of lives and millions of money for the purpose of adding a few more miles of African territory to the British and French Empires."[80]

A reply to the general staff memorandum was not long in coming. Two weeks later, the Admiralty provided a point-by-point refutation. The Admiralty asserted that the primary purpose of the German colonies always had been "to obtain a dominating position in the politics of the world." Not only did they allow Germany to meddle in colonial affairs, but "her colonial harbours have formed at once bases from which her ships can threaten the commerce of other nations and the excuse to her own people for the large expenditure on her navy."[81] Should Germany's colonies be returned, and bases for submarines and cruisers established in them, the colonies would pose an even greater threat to the empire's commerce.

Moving beyond strictly naval considerations, the memorandum provided further criticism of the arguments in support of German colonialism presented by the general staff. The reemergence of a strong Germany was rejected in favor of continued friendly relations among the Allies. In addition, the colonies were shown not to have been outlets for Germany's surplus population, and it was argued that the attachment of the German people to their colonies was in no way comparable to that of the French to Alsace-Lorraine.

---

[80] Ibid.

[81] "Remarks by the Admiralty on the Note by the General Staff as to the Policy to be pursued in regard to the German Colonies", T.C. 10, September 22, 1916, CAB 16/36/66737, PRO.

The Admiralty's arguments appear more in harmony with the mainstream of British colonial thinking. Predicated on German defeat or at least a peace concluded by Britain from a position of advantage, they were much closer to the eventual settlement than those of the general staff. Had there been a negotiated peace, however, opposition to continuing the war for colonial territories certainly would have been more widespread.

The economic repercussions that could result if Cameroon changed hands were addressed in a report to the subcommittee by the Board of Trade. It acknowledged that German colonial tariffs were moderate and contained no preferential treatment for German goods. From the viewpoint of British exporters, this compared favorably with France's varying colonial tariffs. This was particularly significant in relation to Cameroon. Although in 1912 Cameroon's total imports were less than those of German East Africa (£1,684,000 compared with £2,474,000), Britain's exports to Cameroon were greater in value than its exports to all the other German colonies in Africa combined. "The safeguarding of existing British trade is therefore of most importance in exactly that colony which is most likely to pass out of British hands into those of our Allies," observed the author from the Board of Trade.[82]

For the United Kingdom, an "open door" policy in the former German territories was seen as the best option. Unfortunately this policy would encounter the opposition of the Dominions, which appeared determined to apply tariff preferences in the territories they occupied. The Board of Trade suggested that "a general agreement limited to Equatorial Africa" was

---

[82] "British Trade Interests in the German Overseas Possessions," T.C. 15, Board of Trade, October 10, 1916, Cab 16/36/66737, PRO. According to the appendix, the United Kingdom's exports to the German colonies in 1912 were as follows: Cameroon, £272,000; German East Africa, £122,000; Togo, £94,000; and German Southwest Africa, £16,000. However, there were also considerable exports from India to German East Africa, the Gold Coast to Togo and "British South Africa" to German Southwest Africa.

the remaining alternative for protecting British trade. "Only by some such comprehensive arrangement could we hope to induce France to abandon in the Cameroons (if they be ceded to her) the right to accord preference to national goods, which we intend to maintain in South-West Africa."[83]

It is worthwhile to take note of this proposal because the tariff structure of the postwar African mandate system resembled it closely. In what became the class B mandates of equatorial Africa, equal commercial opportunity was decreed, while in the class C mandates, which included German Southwest Africa, the mandatories were allowed to apply their own laws, and consequently, their own tariff preferences. Whatever other reasons may be encountered in support of this system, the Board of Trade memorandum provides evidence of a British economic incentive.

The views of the Colonial Office offered still other arguments for not returning Cameroon to Germany. A supplementary memorandum submitted to the subcommittee noted that the British forces employed in Cameroon had come from West Africa, primarily Nigeria. In Nigeria, the authors maintained, "The Chiefs, both Mohammedan and Pagan, are accustomed to see the conqueror take over the land of the conquered, and the general opinion would no doubt be that, whatever we might say, we had not beaten the Germans."[84] This would result in a "very severe blow to British prestige," forcing a reevaluation of British military policy in a protectorate where there were no European troops.

As the subcommittee was proceeding with its work, the Asquith cabinet resigned, on December 4, 1916. This was followed by Lloyd George's formation of a small war cabinet, aimed at conducting the war effort with more efficiency. At

---

[83] Ibid.

[84] "Memorandum by the Colonial Office," November 3, 1916, CAB 16/36/66737, PRO.

this time, too, the Dominions were demanding a greater role in policy formation. In particular, the southern Dominions insisted upon the retention of the German colonies that their troops had conquered. The British government acknowledged the force of this demand.[85]

One effect of this Dominion input was to accentuate the British inclination to assign expansion in tropical Africa a lower priority than other acquisitions which could be made by the British Empire. This corresponds with explanations for earlier British imperialism that attribute considerable responsibility for Britain's continuing annexation of new overseas territories to the demands of existing possessions. Having rallied to Britain's assistance during the war, the Dominions expected their interests to be placed at the forefront of Britain's territorial objectives.

Recognizing their military contributions, Lloyd George also sought to involve the Dominions more directly in the decision-making process. Consequently, in the spring of 1917, representatives of the self-governing Dominions and India met with members of the British cabinet to participate in the conduct of the war. Organized as the Imperial War Cabinet, this body continued to meet from March 20 until May 2, 1917. As could be expected, the Imperial War Cabinet took a keen interest in colonial questions. On April 20 it created a committee to consider "territorial desiderata" in the future peace settlement. This committee, chaired by Lord Curzon, considered the interim reports of the Mallet subcommittee, but its membership gave it a position of greater political significance. Yet in relation to Germany's African colonies, its recommendations did not differ substantially from the preceding ones.[86] Priority was

---

[85] William Roger Louis, *Great Britain and Germany's Lost Colonies, 1914-1919* (Oxford: Clarendon Press, 1967), p. 78.

[86] This analysis of British aims differs from Lloyd George's later recollection of the committee's work, about which he wrote: "This was the first occasion on which any indication was given that Britain meant as a condi-

placed on German Southwest and East Africa, with Cameroon and Togo seen as available for compensating France.

Discussion of the disposition of Togo and Cameroon occurred at the committee's second meeting, on April 18. There was no extended debate; rather, the committee considered the work of the Mallet subcommittee, focusing on Colonial Office memoranda.

Provided the Allies ended the war in an advantageous position, the subcommittee opposed restoring the colonies to Germany. The members contemplated the acquisition of Togo and Cameroon by France in the final settlement, although with regard to Togo, French intentions were not completely clear. Britain's minimum demands in both colonies required boundary rectifications aimed at uniting border-straddling African ethnic groups under British rule.

Duala remained a point of fundamental concern. Colonial Secretary Walter Long repeated the navy's assessment of its strategic value, "commanding the sea routes to South Africa, and capable of being made almost impregnable." Lord Robert Cecil, parliamentary undersecretary for foreign affairs, commented that Britain "might still conceivably get Duala from the French as part of the general settlement." To Admiral Wilson, it could become "a very great inconvenience" in French hands, but the situation would be much more unfavorable if it were returned to Germany.[87]

At this point General Smuts stated South Africa's priorities, in effect recalling attention to Britain's traditional policy:

> ... if it were a choice between keeping German
> East Africa or the German West African colonies,

---

tion of peace to retain its conquests in the German Colonial Empire." *War Memoirs of David Lloyd George*, 2 vols. (London: Odhams Press, 1942), 1:1037.

[87] Minutes of the meeting of April 18, 1917, Committee on Terms of Peace (Territorial Desiderata), CAB 21/77/66831, PRO.

he considered it much more important to make sure of the safety of the eastern route from South Africa, more particularly as the retention of German East Africa included the provision of a land communication with Egypt, and also secured the Red Sea route to India.[88]

---

[88] Ibid.

3

East Africa:
British and Belgian Interests

Britain's Strategic Concerns

When British statesmen and colonial enthusiasts turned covetous eyes toward East Africa during the late nineteenth century, strategic considerations loomed large in their visions. After the British invasion of Egypt in 1882, British officials became increasingly concerned with control of the upper reaches of the Nile. According to the well-known thesis advanced by Ronald Robinson and John Gallagher, the British occupation of Egypt and the desire to protect British trade routes to India provided critical incentives for acquisitions in East Africa.[1]

The Robinson and Gallagher thesis also suggests that British preoccupation with East Africa disposed them to accommodate French ambitions in West Africa. "Nothing is more striking about the selection of British claims in tropical Africa between 1882 and 1895 than the emphasis on the east and the comparative indifference to the west."[2] Salisbury's 1890 agreement with the French, in which Britain recognized French rights in much of Western and central Africa and Madagascar in return for the acknowledgment of its protectorate over Zanzibar and Pemba, reflects this sense of priorities.

---

[1] Ronald Robinson and John Gallagher with Alice Denny, *Africa and the Victorians: The Climax of Imperialism* (New York: St. Martin's Press, 1961; reprint ed., Garden City, N.Y.: Anchor Books, 1968), pp. 462-467.

[2] Ibid., p. 393.

Although competing prewar colonial aims had been settled diplomatically, German East Africa represented a logical target for Britain in its quest to achieve superiority along the East African littoral. The German colony also conflicted with another enterprise that would resurface in the dreams of British imperialists. This was the Cape-to-Cairo railway scheme of Cecil Rhodes and other expansionists. Pushing north from South Africa, the British reached the eastern shore of Lake Malawi (Nyasa) and claimed the Stevenson Road, which would connect the area with the southern end of Lake Tanganyika. The prospect of developing steamer service on Lake Tanganyika opened the possibility of extending British communications and transport a further 400 miles to the north. At the lake's northern end, only 200 miles separated this visionary British trade route from British claims in Uganda; and from Uganda, communication through the Sudan to Egypt could be imagined.

The Heligoland agreement of 1890 between Britain and Germany foreclosed this possibility. Britain received Uganda, but its southern border west of Lake Victoria was set at one degree south of the equator, thereby sacrificing the corridor to Lake Tanganyika necessary for the Cape-to-Cairo route.[3]

As the First World War progressed these former British aims would reassert themselves. But in East Africa, as on the continent's west coast, the initial wartime objectives of British decision makers were of a limited military character. They sought to disrupt German communications and deny German commerce raiders safe ports.

---

[3] Robert O. Collins, "The Origins of the Nile Struggle: Anglo-German Negotiations and the Mackinnon Agreement of 1890," in *Britain and Germany in Africa: Imperial Rivalry and Colonial Rule*, ed. Prosser Gifford and William Roger Louis (New Haven: Yale University Press, 1967), pp. 119-151. Although Prime Minister Salisbury had endorsed efforts by Mackinnon to obtain from Leopold II access to the lake through the Congo, he was less than enthusiastic about the continental railway idea.

These aims had provided the original motivation for dispatching Indian troops to East Africa. At first assigned the task of capturing Dar es Salaam, the Indian expeditionary force found its mission expanded to denying the Germans the use of any potential naval base along the East African coast. "From that it was but a short step to the prospect of ultimately seizing the whole German protectorate; and it was on this basis, apparently with no realization of the magnitude of such a task and certainly with no adequate regard to ways and means, that the instructions for Major-General Aitken [the British commander] were drawn up."[4]

The failure of the assault on Tanga in November 1914 created fresh concerns for British policy makers. First, there was the question of whether Britain should seek the assistance of its European allies in defeating the Germans in East Africa. The natural sources for such cooperation were the French colony of Madagascar, the Belgian Congo and possibly Portuguese Mozambique.

In response to a British inquiry, the French actually considered which of their military units could be used in East Africa.[5] They were, in fact, quite willing to provide military assistance there and later sought to use their offer to gain British concessions on the continent's west coast. Given Doumergue's attitudes and preparation of the offer, it would not be unreasonable to assume that territorial compensation was also an initial consideration.

---

[4] Hordern, *Official History of the War: Military Operations East Africa*, p. 65.

[5] Le Ministre des colonies à monsieur le Ministre des affaires étrangères, 1 décembre 1914, 1545, La Série Guerre 1914-1918, AMAE,F. In this memorandum Doumergue provided a detailed accounting of troops which would be available for service in East Africa. Beyond those available in Madagascar, he identified several Senegalese battalions which could be sent.

Britain, however, was quick to delay the proffered assistance. The British ambassador wrote to the French foreign minister on December 4, 1914,

> the position in East Africa is not pressing and, as that is so, it appears to them that it would not be advisable that troops should be sent either from France at the present juncture, or from West Africa where all the available troops seem to be required.[6]

The message concluded with the proviso that should the French troops in Madagascar be needed in the future, the British government would again confer with the French.

Collaboration with the Belgians in East Africa was both an earlier and a more pressing matter. Skirmishes along the Belgian Congo's border with German East Africa took place during the opening weeks of the war. In September 1914, British positions south of Lake Tanganyika appeared seriously threatened and, to local British officials, nearby troops in the Congo offered logical reinforcements.[7]

Later during the month, it was suggested from South Africa that a larger force from the Congo could be used in offensive operations against the German position at Bismarckburg on

---

[6] British ambassador to the French foreign minister, December 5, 1914, 1545, La Série Guerre 1914-1918, AMAE,F.

[7] Paraphrase telegram, The High Commissioner for South Africa to the Secretary of State for the Colonies, received September 17, 1914, Davidson Papers, Colonial Office Box, East Africa 1914-15, House of Lords Record Office, London (HLRO). The telegram offers the following description of events: "A civil servant in Northern Rhodesia, it appears, asked without authority for Belgian troops to co-operate on the north eastern border. These troops have started and the Commandant General does not consider that they can be stopped without friction being caused and had given instructions to Major Stennett to see that their actions conform to our instructions to remain for the present on the defensive."

Lake Tanganyika.[8] This proposal met heated opposition from Colonial Secretary Harcourt. He responded:

> From a political point of view it is eminently undesirable to have Belgians taking part in operations against German Colonies in Africa either by themselves or in co-operation with British Forces, and you should endeavour to discourage such action as far as possible. I must leave to your discretion what reasons should be given such as lack of supplies, or others.[9]

Correspondingly the proposed action was abandoned.

During the previous month the prospect of military cooperation with the Portuguese also had been rejected. Following a discussion of the issue by Harcourt and Foreign Secretary Grey, the governor of Nyasaland was advised: "In view of European political considerations you should not ask for or accept Portuguese assistance without instructions from His Majesty's Government."[10] This may be explained in part because Portugal was officially neutral until March 9, 1916. Germany declared war only after the Portuguese had followed a British request and seized German vessels in Portuguese waters. Yet fighting in Angola between the Portuguese and the Germans began as early as October 1914. In Africa, a state of belligerency between the two countries seems to have existed long before the official declaration of war.[11]

---

[8] Paraphrase telegram, The Governor-General of the Union of South Africa to the Secretary of State for the Colonies, September 21, 1914, ibid.

[9] Paraphrase telegram, The Secretary of State for the Colonies to the High Commissioner of South Africa, September 22, 1914, ibid.

[10] Paraphrase telegram, The Secretary of State for the Colonies to the Governor of Nyasaland Protectorate, August 22, 1914, ibid.

[11] Douglas L. Wheeler, *Republican Portugal: A Political History 1910-1926* (Madison: University of Wisconsin Press, 1978), pp. 127-128.

From the very outset of the war, then, Britain appeared to adopt a policy of seeking to restrict the conflict in East Africa to a unilateral confrontation with the Germans. This reflected the priority British decision makers placed on having a free hand in determining the future of East Africa, although initially there were other considerations too. These involved the questions of Portugal's and the Belgian Congo's neutrality as well as the rationale that there were more pressing needs for French colonial troops in other theaters.

A second, and related, concern of paramount importance to the British was how Africans would react to war among the European powers. Ambassador Bertie had used anxiety over the issue as justification for Britain acting alone, explaining to the French that the presence of a third power might increase the danger of agitation among the local population.[12] This concern was particularly acute in East and central Africa.

Elsewhere in Africa, other factors had partially alleviated the repercussions of using the continent as a battleground for European antagonists. In German Southwest Africa and along the coast of Cameroon there was more African animosity toward German rule than in most of their East African colony. The Allied operations on Africa's west coast were also of a shorter duration, and those in southwest Africa principally pitted white South Africans against German troops.

In the East African theater, the attitudes of the indigenous populations on both sides of the colonial borders attracted sustained British interest. British officials suspected, and hoped, that African resentment toward German colonial rule would disrupt the German war effort. At the same time, there was fear that the fighting might undercut the foundations of colonial rule throughout the region.

---

[12] "Visite de Sir Fr. Bertie, action dans l'Est Allemand pour Dar es Salaam," Affaires étrangères, Cabinet du ministre, Paris, August 13, 1914, 1545, La Série Guerre 1914-1918, AMAE,F.

Unfortunately, from the British viewpoint, prewar African discontent in the German colony failed to interfere seriously with the conduct of the war. In fact, the African soldiers in particular remained loyal to their German officers. Subsequently, this raised an issue that complicated British efforts to justify their acquisition of the colony by claiming that such a transfer of colonial rule represented the desires of the African population.

At the outbreak of the war, the attitudes of Africans in the British colonies were also a pressing concern for the Colonial Office. On August 23, 1914, for example, the governor of East Africa reported to London that "the Giriame tribe near MALINDI had taken advantage of the situation and were preparing for an organized attack on Europeans." The message continued that as a response, "two companies K.A.R. [King's African Rifles] had been sent to take drastic action and to quell any signs of disaffection."[13]

Giriame grievances were not simply the result of German intrigue. The tribe had resisted closer British administration since 1912. Defeated by British colonial forces on August 28, 1914, the Giriame were compelled to agree to a fine of 100,000 rupees (approximately £6,600) and to provide one thousand men for the carrier corps. They avoided doing both until a punitive expedition was sent against them, and many of the carriers who finally were recruited deserted.[14]

Even more disquieting to the British was the revolt of John Chilembwe in Nyasaland. Before the war, Chilembwe had studied at a black Baptist seminary in the United States and returned to found a mission in Nyasaland. There he became increasingly disturbed by the harsh working conditions of Africans on European estates and troubled by his personal problems. With the spread of the war to Africa, he perceived

---

[13] "Operations in East Africa," Harcourt Papers, 508:312, BLO.

[14] Savage and Munro, "Carrier Corps Recruitment," 7:318.

new suffering for his countrymen in the growing demands for soldiers and carriers. Finally, these combined grievances caused him to lead an insurrection in January 1915. At the same time, he secretly sought German support.[15]

The fighting was not protracted. Although the rebels killed only three Europeans, and Chilembwe issued orders for humane behavior by his followers, the rising was suppressed brutally. Within two months Chilembwe and forty of his supporters had been shot or hanged.

The number of casualties was not large compared with other instances of conflict between Africans and European imperialists. Yet the revolt had a powerful effect. Historically, Chilembwe has been portrayed as representative of a new, forward-looking African patriotism which cut across tribal lines.[16] In early 1915 the British saw in the incident the frightening vision of local problems combining with the destabilizing wartime conditions to undermine their colonial rule.

In a message to Harcourt on January 26, the governor of Nyasaland described the revolt as a "serious outbreak of natives" which he believed had made it "necessary to invoke the assistance of Portuguese troops." Three weeks later, he reported that "as a result of a further enquiry into the recent rebellion there were indications of far-reaching causes and widespread disaffection."[17] Further, he thought the dispatch of Indian troops to the protectorate was necessary to prevent a

---

[15] Shepperson and Price, *Independent African*, pp. 256-258. See also Melvin E. Page, "The War of Thangata: Nyasaland and the East African Campaign, 1914-1918," *Journal of African History*, 19, 1 (1978):87-100 for a detailed account of the hardships the war brought to the region and the various methods of African resistance.

[16] Shepperson and Price, *Independent African*, pp. 408-409.

[17] "Colonial Office: Operations in British Dominions and Colonies and German Territories," 1915, Harcourt Papers, 509:185-187, BLO.

recurrence of the revolt and to reassure the European inhabitants.[18]

The development of East African policy in London did not remain focused on the Chilembwe uprising, but neither was the incident easily forgotten by Colonial Office officials dealing with the region. The uprising gives British arguments that the Germans were unfit colonial rulers a hypocritical ring. Not only did many Africans remain loyal to the Germans, but in Nyasaland and elsewhere Africans revolted against oppressive *Allied* policies.

Enunciating the Empire's Objectives

The development of long-range British policy toward East Africa reflects a combination of prewar tendencies, military-strategic concerns and new economic opportunities. The appetite for aggrandizement that these produced was complemented and justified by an appeal to imperial and African interests.

Relatively early in the war, the value of acquiring German East Africa was recognized by the Colonial Office. In March 1915, Harcourt's memorandum, "The Spoils," listed the advantages that this acquisition would bring to the British Empire. It was a missive of old visions, imperial interests and an unambiguous economic justification for colonial expansion.

> German East Africa forms the missing link in the chain of British possessions from the Cape to Cairo.

---

[18] Ibid., 509:194-195. As late as July, the governor still was requesting that outside troops be sent. He reported that "there were grounds for uneasiness in the present attitude of the natives in NYASALAND and in the adjoining Portuguese territory. . . . The situation turned entirely on the loyalty of the native troops, . . . " Harcourt responded by ruling out Indian and British troops but encouraging South Africa to send reinforcements.

It would make an admirable colony for Indian emigration of the class which wants to trade
not to cultivate, assuming that the latter will be
provided for in Mesopotamia.

The German railway, now complete, from Ujiji
on Lake Tanganyika to Dar-es-Salaam on the coast,
will in future tap and carry a large part of the
trade of the Belgian Congo, and will deprive our
Uganda Railway of much of the traffic which it
now obtains from Ruanda and the southern half
of Victoria Nyanza.[19]

Two years later, a full exposition of the growing British motives for retaining German East Africa appeared in the second
interim report of the Mallet Committee (the interdepartmental
subcommittee on territorial changes of the Committee of Imperial Defence). Here military and strategic issues were given
the special prominence they usually command in the midst of a
war. The fighting was continuing in East Africa, and each difficulty the British encountered seemed to provide an additional
reason for not returning the colony to Germany.

In describing the conquest of the German colonies, the report observes, "from the German point of view, indeed, the
operations in Africa can only be regarded as a military diver-
sion of the most successful character." As a result, the subcommittee concluded that it was "clearly undesirable to risk
incurring similar sacrifices and difficulties in the conceivable
event of another war."[20]

The Admiralty expressed particular concern over the threat
to Allied shipping posed by a return of Germany's African
colonies. The *Königsberg* had forced the British navy to main-

---

[19] "The Spoils," p. 2, CAB 37/126/66620, PRO.

[20] "Second Interim Report of the Sub-Committee on Territorial Changes,"
March 22, 1917, p. 2, CAB 16/36/66737, PRO.

tain a watch on the Rufiji River for nine months.[21] Disquieting as this episode was by itself, the successes of German submarines in the North Atlantic caused it to appear even more serious. It was predicted that submarine bases would be established on both coasts of Africa and that the "immunity" of Allied vessels in the Indian Ocean and the South Atlantic would cease to exist.

German East Africa also posed a regional military threat that Britain could end by retaining the colony after the war. The effect of von Lettow-Vorbeck's raids on the Mombasa-Nairobi railway during 1915 is apparent in the observation that "the annexation of German East Africa would eliminate an indefensible frontier of 550 miles in immediate proximity to our main artery of communications in British East Africa."[22] Moreover, such an acquisition would have meant that Britain's colonies in central and East Africa had only "unaggressive States like Portugal and Belgium" as neighbors.

The report revived and endorsed the dream of British territory stretching from the Cape to Cairo. In doing so, it gave a new dimension to railway schemes: "the Committee wish more particularly, in view of the experience of the present war, to lay stress on the military importance of linking up the different portions of the British Empire by railway, wherever possible."[23]

Despite this natural preoccupation with military affairs during wartime, economic considerations were not omitted. German East Africa was described as the richest of Germany's colonies. A land with extensive mineral resources, it also contained great agricultural potential. Here, at least in the context of developing these resources, German colonialism was not reviled. Rather it was pointed out that "a great deal of useful

---

[21] Ibid.

[22] Ibid., p. 3.

[23] Ibid., p. 4.

experimental and pioneer work has been done by the Germans, the benefit of which will be reaped by their successors."[24]

There appeared to be attractive possibilities for immigration to East Africa. Highland areas were considered suitable for European settlement. In addition, the report recognized the legitimacy of accommodating some form of Indian immigration.

The latter policy had been advocated in a dispatch from the government of India in September 1916. It argued that Indian interests in retaining territories captured from the enemy were limited to Iraq and German East Africa. Indian colonization of Iraq, however, was likely to encounter difficulties. Correspondingly, the importance that "Indian expansion should find an outlet in German East Africa" was increased.

India's British rulers saw in German East Africa a marvelous opportunity to deal with the "surplus population" of the subcontinent. "No other territory is so suitable for Indian colonisation, none other so convenient of access, and there is already a considerable Indian population settled in the vicinity," affirmed the voice of Britain's colonial administrators.[25]

Beyond the government of India, the subcommittee acknowledged that there were other parts of the British Empire entitled to a role in deciding the future of German East Africa. Both the Union of South Africa and British East Africa had made military contributions to the ongoing conquest of the German colony. Returning the colony to Germany, the report alleged, would "create profound disappointment in the Union" and "be even more keenly resented by the white community of British East Africa."[26]

---

[24] Ibid., p. 5.

[25] "Extract from Secret Letter from the Government of India," T.C. 19, September 29, 1916, CAB 16/36/67737, PRO.

[26] "Second Interim Report of the Sub-Committee on Territorial Changes," p. 5.

This professed respect for the interests of the British Empire's member states also characterized the work of the Curzon Committee (Committee on Terms of Peace [Territorial Desiderata] of the Imperial War Cabinet) in April 1917. As in the case of West Africa, the Curzon Committee reached conclusions that generally reinforced the East African policy articulated by the Mallet Committee.

These recommendations of the Curzon Committee were embodied in a series of resolutions summarizing their deliberations. Returning German East Africa to German rule, they advised, "would involve a grave political and military menace to the British possessions adjoining it, and would make possible the establishment of a formidable German naval base in the Indian Ocean which would threaten both the Cape and the Red Sea routes to the East."[27] Further, by retaining the German colony, the British Empire would gain the additional benefit of "direct territorial continuity" between its African components. As a result of these considerations, British retention was viewed as "an object of the first consequence."

The discussions leading to the formulation of these policy guidelines had taken place at the committee's first meeting, on April 17, 1917. There Lord Curzon had described the military dangers associated with a return of the Germans to East Africa. Then the chairman, along with Austen Chamberlain, the secretary of state for India, had emphasized the potential utility of the colony as a site for future Indian immigration. Next the chairman, now joined by Walter Long, the colonial secretary, pointed out the presumably negative effect a reversion to German rule would have on "the minds of natives," both inside the colony and elsewhere in Africa.[28] General Smuts asserted that

---

[27] "Report of Committee on Terms of Peace (Territorial Desiderata)," April 28, 1917, CAB 21/77/66831, PRO.

[28] Minutes of the meeting of April 17, 1917, Committee on Terms of Peace (Territorial Desiderata), CAB 21/77/66831, PRO. The Curzon Committee submitted the minutes of their meetings together with their conclu-

"German designs of creating a great Central African Empire" constituted an additional peril.

In a new twist to Cape-to-Cairo railroad schemes, Smuts cautioned that the most direct route to Uganda was blocked by the mountainous territory north of Lake Tanganyika, making it necessary to find an alternate route. This, he confidently proposed, could be done by using the existing German railway from Ujiji, on Lake Tanganyika, to Tabora. From Tabora a line, already planned by the Germans, would be constructed to Mwanza on Lake Victoria. It was thus "essential to retain at any rate that part of German East Africa which lay to the west of that line."[29]

A glance at the map of German East Africa will quickly reveal that Smuts's railway proposal would have required a much greater cession by Germany than had earlier railroad plans, in which the line would have been hundreds of miles to the west. The implication, however, that some of the colony could be returned to Germany may have prompted an inquiry from committee member Lord Robert Cecil. Referring to the Second Interim Report of the Mallet Committee, he asked if this might not be possible.

The earlier subcommittee had considered the subject in the event that Britain was forced to negotiate an unsatisfactory peace. Under such circumstances it had ranked the order in which colonies might be returned to Germany. First had been Togo, followed by Cameroon; but these were obviously limited sacrifices, since it was anticipated that they would be assigned to France. "If the situation at the end of the war is so unsatisfactory that even these concessions are insufficient, it might then be necessary to face the possibility of having to surrender the south-eastern portion of German East Africa,

---

sions, believing that the former were necessary for completely understanding the latter.

[29] Ibid.

including the ports of Lindi and Kilwa, and, if it came to the worst, Dar es Salaam."[30]

In the Curzon Committee, however, the retrocession of any part of East Africa to Germany after the war met a cold reception. Smuts argued that "the best harbour in the whole of East Africa" lay south of Dar es Salaam. Furthermore, he believed that the Germans had chosen this site, at Kilwa Kiswani, for a future naval base.[31]

When Cecil suggested that with the colony's size greatly reduced, it might be possible to capture a naval base from land, Sir S. Sinha, the Indian representative, responded that the Germans would seek to retain a small colony only for "the mischief they might be able to do with their naval base." Smuts now added that no partition of the colony was likely to prove satisfactory. Chamberlain and Long joined in, reiterating admonitions against a future German naval base.

Consequently, the committee concluded that it was "essential to retain the whole of German East Africa in British possession" and stated that if German East Africa was to be compared from political, strategic and commercial viewpoints with Togo and Cameroon, "there could be no doubt that the former was of far greater importance."[32]

Africans and Allies

Even as the Curzon Committee was meeting, changing circumstances and popular attitudes were propelling debate over Germany's colonies in new directions. Strategic and economic interests continued to direct the war aims of Allied statesmen,

---

[30] "Second Interim Report of the Sub-Committee on Territorial Changes," p. 6.

[31] Minutes of the meeting of April 17, 1917, Committee on Terms of Peace (Territorial Desiderata).

[32] Ibid.

but it became necessary to provide an altruistic public justification for colonial expansion. The alleged African preference for rule by Britain, France and Belgium seemed to offer the requisite vindication. All three countries eventually adopted this rationale, but the British, who were most keenly concerned with colonial issues, placed the greatest emphasis on it.

Behind the public declaration of war aims by the British government pressed a combination of military stalemate and new ideological challenges. In the fall of 1917 the Battle of Passchendaele left Britain with close to 500,000 casualties for the gain of small, inconsequential territory. Despondency spread among the British troops, duplicating the disillusionment of the French army brought on by the Nivelle offensive.

This mood was not prevalent only among the soldiers. "The war fever had burnt itself out long ago in every warring country," wrote Lloyd George of the common European war-weariness at the outset of 1918.[33] In this atmosphere imperialist aims were likely to encounter a hostile reception. Further, new ideological challenges to the old diplomacy intensified popular support for moral peace terms.

Under pressure from the Petrograd Soviet, the provisional government of Russia had in the spring of 1917 adopted a public policy of peace without annexations or indemnities.[34] Among large sectors of Europe's population, particularly on the left, this appeal touched an emotional chord. After seizing control in November, the Bolsheviks reaffirmed the call for "a democratic peace on the basis of no annexations or indemnities and the self-determination of nations."[35]

---

[33] *War Memoirs of David Lloyd George*, 2 vols. (London: Odhams Press, 1942), 2:1467.

[34] Rex A. Wade, *The Russian Search for Peace, February-October 1917* (Stanford: Stanford University Press, 1969), pp. 26-50.

[35] Leon Trotsky, "Note of Foreign Minister Trotsky to the Allied Embassies in Petrograd Offering an Armistice," November 21, 1917, *Official*

Carrying the last of these points beyond almost all other parties at the time, the Bolsheviks argued that the concept of self-determination should be extended to peoples living under European colonial rule.[36]

Soviet publication of the secret Allied treaties reinforced the perception that imperialist rivalries were behind the war. With regard to Africa, the Treaty of London, under which Italy had entered the war in 1915, appeared to contain a glaring acknowledgement that a repartition of colonial empires was under consideration. Article Thirteen of the treaty promised that Italy would be given territorial compensation in Africa if Britain and France expanded their empires by annexing Germany's colonies.[37]

A second challenge to British colonial expansion came from across the Atlantic. In his famous address to the United States Senate on January 22, 1917, President Woodrow Wilson called for "peace without victory."[38] Wilson proposed a peace based

---

Statements of War Aims and Peace Proposals: December 1916 to November 1918, prepared under the supervision of James Brown Scott (Washington, D.C.: Carnegie Endowment for International Peace, 1921), pp. 188-189.

[36] Arno J. Mayer, *Political Origins of the New Diplomacy, 1917-1918* (New York: Howard Fertig, 1969), p. 298. According to Mayer: "It was through Bolshevik insistence at Brest-Litovsk that self-determination became a 'dominant interest' for the diplomacy of the war." Further, he points out that the Bolshevik application of self-determination to colonial areas was "a major deviation from the Western program." It was not, however, one which could be ignored.

[37] Robert L. Hess, "Italy and Africa: Colonial Ambitions in the First World War," *Journal of African History* 5 (1963):105-126 provides a full account of Italy's colonial aims in Africa during the war and the peace conference. Hess points out the growing concern of Italian Colonial Minister Gaspare Colosimo that the changing wartime atmosphere would threaten Italy's colonial ambitions.

[38] "Address of the President of the United States to the Senate, January 22, 1917," U.S. Department of State, *Papers Relating to the Foreign*

upon the principle of self-determination, but he did not envision the concept as an endorsement for the liberation of all colonial peoples. When he first included the concept as an essential ingredient for a just peace, it appears he had not considered all its ramifications.[39] Later, when he did apply it to colonial peoples, as in Article Five of his Fourteen Points, he limited its scope. There Wilson placed equal emphasis upon the interests of the colonial population and the colonial power in determining the colony's future.[40]

Certainly the anti-imperialist aspects of this program differed from those of the Bolsheviks. Nevertheless, both policies constituted attacks upon the expansionist colonial designs of the belligerent states. If it ever had been possible for British leaders to argue openly that Germany's colonies should be annexed for purely strategic and economic reasons, the time had passed.

Relations of the United States, 1917, Supplement 1, The World War (Washington, D.C.: Government Printing Office, 1931), p. 29. Wilson declared: "I am proposing, as it were, that the nations should with one accord adopt the doctrine of President Monroe as the doctrine of the world: that no nation should seek to extend its polity over any other nation or people, but that every people should be left free to determine its own polity, its own way of development, unhindered, unthreatened, unafraid, the little along with the great and powerful."

[39] Alfred Cobban, *National Self-Determination* (London: Oxford University Press, 1948), p. 21.

[40] "Address of President Wilson on the Conditions of Peace delivered at a Joint Session of the two Houses of Congress," January 8, 1918, Scott, p. 237. Article Five of his peace program reads: "A free, open-minded, and absolutely impartial adjustment of all colonial claims, based upon a strict observance of the principle that in determining all such questions of sovereignty the interests of the populations concerned must have equal weight with the equitable claims of the government whose title is to be determined."

Under these circumstances, it was logical and practical that the public justification for not returning Germany's colonies should focus on the interests of the colonies' inhabitants. This was particularly true in German Southwest and East Africa, where it was possible to produce evidence of German misrule before the war.

Ample British propaganda appeared to encourage the development of these sentiments. An example of this is to be found in the twenty-four page open letter from the bishop of Zanzibar to General Smuts. Dated November 7, 1917, it was printed the following year in pamphlet form by the Universities' Mission to Central Africa under the title: *The Black Slaves of Prussia.*

The broadside presented vivid images of German cruelty. "The German *sjambok* [whip], of rhinoceros or hippopotamus hide, is cut to damage, not merely to hurt," wrote the bishop. After detailing other charges of German abuse he concluded, "let me add that Germans on tour required as a rule to be supplied with a young girl at each sleeping-place."[41] The only humane solution to such conditions was the establishment of British rule.

On the left of the British political spectrum genuine concern for Africans had a more disinterested character. J.A. Hobson and E.D. Morel, leading publicists on European imperial-

---

[41] Frank D.D. Weston, Bishop of Zanzibar, *The Black Slaves of Prussia,* "An Open Letter Addressed to General Smuts," (London: Universities' Mission to Central Africa, 1918), pp. 7 and 11. CO 691/20, PRO. The bishop's concerns may not have been completely altruistic. Anglican missionaries had founded St. Andrews College in Zanzibar, which drew most of its students from German East Africa. The graduates formed a well-educated intelligentsia. The Germans, however, suspected their loyalty and excluded them from administrative offices. See John Iliffe, *Tanganyika under German Rule* (Cambridge: Cambridge University Press, 1969), pp. 174-180.

ism in Africa, led a campaign for international supervision of
colonial rule.[42] By the end of 1917 the Labour Party had placed
tropical Africa within the vanguard of its anti-imperialist peace
program. Writes Arno Mayer, "As a leader of Russia, Lenin
tended to focus on the colonial areas located on the Eurasian
land mass; Labour assigned Africa a central position in its
colonial program."[43]

In August, the Labour Party's executive had proposed a
single, independent African state between the Zambezi and the
Sahara. It was to be placed under the supervision of the future
League of Nations, with free trade and the rights of Africans
guaranteed. On December 28, the party's "Memorandum on
War Aims," including a proposal for the transfer of colonies in
tropical Africa to the administration of the future League of
Nations, was approved by a special labor conference in London.[44] Liberals, too, debated the colonies' future.[45]

Consequently, it is not surprising that imperial representatives and British officials realized that careful consideration
had to be given to how the empire could justify the annexation of the German colonies. Gaddis Smith points out that
while Arthur Henderson of the Labour Party cast the only
vote against accepting the Curzon report in the Imperial War
Cabinet, the Canadian Prime Minister, Sir Robert Borden, declared "that a proposal to add one million square miles to the
British Empire... would be coldly and cynically received by
the world."[46]

---

[42] Laurence W. Martin, *Peace without Victory: Woodrow Wilson and
the British Liberals* (Port Washington, N.Y.: Kennikat Press, 1973), p. 77.

[43] Mayer, *Political Origins of the New Diplomacy*, p. 319.

[44] Henry R. Winkler, "The Idea of Colonial Trusteeship," *The League
of Nations Movement in Great Britain, 1914-1919* (New Brunswick, N.J.:
Rutgers University Press, 1952), pp. 206-208.

[45] Ibid., pp. 218-219.

[46] Gaddis Smith, "The British Government and the Disposition of the
German Colonies in Africa, 1914-1918," *Britain and Germany in Africa,*

Responding to this new political atmosphere, the public discourse of Prime Minister Lloyd George advanced the leitmotif of African interests. Speaking in Glasgow on June 29, 1917, he declared that the question of the German colonies would have to be settled at a peace conference. There "the wishes, desires, and the interests of the people of these countries themselves must be the dominant factor in settling their future government."[47] The prime minister's confident remarks also suggested the predisposed direction of such a settlement. He asked whether the inhabitants would be likely to prefer a return of their former rulers or "trust their destiny to others [with]... juster and – may I confidently say – gentler hands."[48]

During the House of Commons debate on December 20, 1917, Lloyd George promised that a peace congress would settle colonial questions, but on "the principle of respecting the desires of the people themselves." Again, he seemed sure of what this would be in the German colonies, "about which tales are told that make one shudder." There the "poor, helpless people, [were] begging and craving, as they are doing, not to return them to German terrorism."[49]

Less than three weeks later, the prime minister reiterated the theme in a major war aims address to the Trades Union Congress. The German colonies were, as he had announced repeatedly, "held at the disposal of a Conference whose decision must have primary regard to the wishes and interests of the native inhabitants of such colonies."

Continuing his discussion of the topic, Lloyd George argued that it was possible to ascertain African preferences for

---

ed. Gifford and Louis, p. 289.

[47] "Address of Prime Minister Lloyd George at Glasgow on Peace Terms," June 29, 1917, Scott, p. 111.

[48] Ibid.

[49] United Kingdom, *Parliamentary Debates (Commons)*, 5th series, vol. 100 (1917), pp. 2220-2221.

their future government: "The natives live in their various tribal organizations under chiefs and councils who are competent to consult and speak for their tribes and members, and thus to represent their wishes and interests in regard to their disposal."[50]

The German position, that the loyalty of the Africans in the German colonies had been proven by their support during the war, was dismissed by the prime minister. Of all the German colonies it applied, if at all, only to German East Africa. There it represented not the will of the majority but only the support "of a small warlike class from whom their Askaris, or soldiers, were selected." Thus, Lloyd George concluded: "The German treatment of their native populations in their colonies has been such as amply to justify their fear of submitting the future of those colonies to the wishes of the natives themselves."[51]

With this publicly appealing answer to the anti-imperialist policies of Lenin and Wilson, the British government believed it had provided an ethical foundation for the expansion of the empire. If the argument was sincerely intended, however, an African desire for the replacement of German colonial rule with that of other nations should have been manifest.

Unlike West Africa, at the time there was no African-owned press in East Africa which might have voiced the views of at least the indigenous elite.[52] Instead, the British government received a succession of reports from its colonial officials in German East Africa questioning the comfortable assumption of unequivocal African support for British administration.

In June 1917, the British administrator of occupied German territory in East Africa, H.A. Byatt, described conditions

---

[50] "Mr. Lloyd George's Speech to the Trade Unions, January 5, 1918," *War Memoirs of David Lloyd George*, 2:1515.

[51] Ibid., p. 1516.

[52] William A. Hachten, *Muffled Drums: The News Media in Africa* (Ames: Iowa State University Press, 1971), pp. 199-201.

in the town of Bukoba on the shore of Lake Victoria. In general, his report recounted a successful transition to British rule and remarked that the good local relations between the Germans and Africans stood in contrast to those elsewhere. However, of the German system of indirect rule in the area, he wrote:

> The system worked with success, since good relations appear to have existed between the German Government and the Sultanates for some years past, and when the Germans finally evacuated Bukoba their departure was viewed by the natives with some regret. One Sultan is said to have committed suicide, and another, an ardent admirer of German rule, died, fortunately for us, shortly afterwards.[53]

Later that year, Richard Feetham, an officer from southern Africa serving in East Africa, wrote a detailed analysis of considerations bearing on the retention of German East Africa by Britain. Fully favoring British expansion, Feetham nevertheless realized that there would be considerable difficulty in using African wishes as a justification.

"From such casual enquiries as I have had the chance of making it does not seem that on their ante war record in this Territory the case against German rule is very black," wrote Feetham. He believed their most objectionable policy to be that of forced labor. Yet he admitted, "the German requirements for forced labour in peace time were as nothing compared to our war demands."

Although the Masai and some other Africans had supported Britain, Feetham acknowledged that "the general native attitude seems to be one of cold neutrality." Still Britain should make the argument that a return of the territory to Germany

---

[53] "Tour of Inspection to Mwanza and Bukoba," (Report by Mr. Byatt), June 7, 1917, Despatch No. 59, CO 691/5, PRO.

would mean "a betrayal of our friends and grave injury to our good name among African natives."[54]

The following April, Feetham provided an addendum to his earlier report. Addressing in part the question of African opinion, he questioned whether the prime minister's proposals would produce replies favorable to Britain. "From what I could learn it seems that the German method of rule was more acceptable to the Chiefs than to the people."[55] Indirect rule had left the chiefs with considerable freedom, while they passed on the burden of German colonialism to their people. Consequently, "if this was the general position, it will be seen that the opinions of Chiefs will not necessarily be a true indication of the attitude of the mass of the natives towards German rule."

In March 1918, Byatt also produced a comprehensive report on African attitudes toward British rule in the northern area of German East Africa. Certainly, Byatt was not an unbiased observer, and his belief that the inhabitants of the German colony would be better off under British administration characterized the report. He argued that in the districts under British administration, Africans preferred British rule. This alleged preference was based on a more equitable and humane administration of justice and less oppressive taxation.

Byatt's discussion of German colonialism, however, was more circumspect than the denunciations issuing from London, and he was altogether opposed to the application of the idea of self-determination in East Africa. He began by observing that, in his opinion, "it was an error to assume that from the outbreak of war the natives of this country as a whole eagerly looked forward to the possibility of their deliverance by

---

[54] Richard Feetham, "German East Africa," October 2, 1917, CO 691/20/67347, PRO.

[55] "Addendum to Mr. Feetham's memorandum on German East Africa," April 6, 1918, CO 691/20/67347, PRO.

us from the tyrannical rule of the Germans."[56] Indeed, the "exigencies of war" had prevented the rapid establishment of the "popularity of British rule," and in a few places had brought the African population "to the verge of open resistance."

The author's concern with the "exigencies of war" reflected African opposition resulting from the oppressive demands on supplies and labor made by the British forces as well as the Germans. Consequently, Byatt advised, "It would be injudicious to make open and general inquiry of the natives as to whether they prefer British or German rule." Having surveyed his district officers, he found that most of them shared his "views as to the unwisdom of anything in the nature of a plebiscite at the present time, when natives as a whole have not yet had an experience of peaceful British rule long enough to enable them to form a just estimate of its qualities."[57]

The opinions of some informed permanent officials in London also reflected a cautious approach to criticizing German colonialism in East Africa. An example can be seen in a Colonial Office memorandum on the advisability of sending to German East Africa an officer who had prepared a highly critical report on German colonialism in Southwest Africa.[58] Assistant

---

[56] "Correspondence Relating to the Wishes of the Natives of the German Colonies as to their Future Government," Cd. 9210, November 1918, No. 11, German East Africa, March 22, 1918, CAB 29/1/66939, PRO. Byatt's report was included in the above command paper which by means of telegrams, letters and reports sought to show that the indigenous population of the German colonies desired to remain under the rule of Britain and the Dominions.

[57] Ibid.

[58] The Administrator's Office at Windhoek, Southwest Africa, had produced a paper in January 1918 titled "Report on the Natives of South-West Africa and their treatment by Germany." The account provided a long and detailed record of German oppression in the colony. It contained graphic descriptions of hangings and whippings, supported by a large number of eyewitness accounts. There can be little doubt that the aim of the report

Colonial Undersecretary Sir H.J. Read argued that such an action would be inappropriate. Attacking a comparison between German Southwest and East Africa, he pointed out the divergent course which German colonialism in East Africa had followed:

> As a matter of fact the cases are entirely different. The affaire Peters is stale by now and the old conditions were duly condemned by the Reichstag; and however great the severity with which the 1905-6 rebellion was put down there was nothing between 1907 & the outbreak of war at all comparable with the state of affairs in S. W. Africa.[59]

Here again is equivocation in a British appraisal of German colonialism in East Africa. The ambivalent position of some British officials is evident. There was near-universal agreement among them that British rule was better than German. In East Africa, however, it seemed questionable whether the extent of German misrule would justify the confiscation of the colony; nor was it clear that the African population had yet realized the assumed superiority of British rule. A perhaps more insightful analysis of the situation was offered by Charles Dundas, a British officer charged with producing an indictment of German rule: "If the truth were known, the native might have said the equivalent of 'A plague on both your houses.'"[60]

The question of African preferences also contained another component. During the last years of the war, it appeared increasingly possible that Belgium would acquire Urundi and Ruanda. Though British officials were having difficulty in

---

was to prevent any return of the colony to Germany.

[59] "Future of (German) East Africa," cover comments by H. J. Read, June 29, 1918, CO 532/111/67208, PRO.

[60] Sir Charles Dundas, *African Crossroads* (London: Macmillan and Co., 1955), p. 106.

reaching a final verdict on German colonialism in East Africa, there was near unanimity in their criticism of Belgian colonial administration in the territory during the war.[61]

Numerous field reports described the Belgian colonial troops' lack of discipline. In October 1917, W.E. Owen, acting chaplain of the British lake forces in East Africa, described how local women were being seized by troops from the Congo, apparently with their Belgian officers' approval.[62] That same month the brigadier general of the lake force wrote of the behavior of the Belgian colonial troops: "This wholesale ravage, theft and rape is so serious a matter that it is certain to become known in Europe with what effect I leave others to judge."[63]

In June 1917, when a German raiding party slipped back into the northwestern part of the colony, Belgian colonial troops had to be employed against it. The report on their performance by the British district officer at Mwanza, H.M. Tugnell, was strikingly similar to those preceding it.

> From an Administrative point of view no great-
> er disaster could well have happened than that
> Belgian troops should have been employed to deal
> with the enemy in a District which was settling
> down well and where satisfactory progress was

---

[61] Negative evaluations of Belgian colonial rule were not limited to wartime comparisons. In an example reflecting a great part of British thinking, Feetham wrote: "Among those Englishmen who have been in contact with Portuguese or Belgian native administration the opinion seems to be strongly held that whatever the defects of German administration [the natives] would on the past record of the powers concerned be decide[d]ly worse off under either Belgians or Portuguese." "German East Africa," CO 691/20/67347, PRO.

[62] W.E. Owen to Lieutenant Colonel Wilkinson, Ingalula, October 1, 1916, FO 371/2857, PRO.

[63] Brigadier General to Captain Nugent, Ndala, October 4, 1916, FO 371/2857, PRO.

being made. These troops appear to be an absolutely uncontrolled and undisciplined mob, who rape and loot in every direction, and it is now almost impossible to get into touch with the natives at all in those areas through which they have passed. I have not so far heard any complaints of outrages committed by the German Column and it cannot therefore be a matter of surprise if the Natives assist the Germans and fail to supply us with information as to their movements.[64]

Nor should it be thought that officials in London were unfamiliar with these opinions from East Africa. In October 1917, the minutes of a Foreign Office covering memorandum warned that a "clever move" by the Germans would be a campaign to discredit Belgian and Portuguese rule for the purpose of redistributing European colonies in Africa. "Unfortunately," continued the analysis, "there is a great mass of evidence from less tainted sources showing that the Belgians have often not had their colonial troops under control."[65]

Despite the foregoing views, British leaders proved reluctant, but willing to allow a large part of the population in German East Africa to pass under Belgian rule. This decision illustrates the divergence of the public and confidential government priorities attached to African interests. In public, perceived African preferences were among the principal justifications for the confiscation of Germany's colonies at the end of the war. Yet the actual repartition of the continent would reflect the competition and conciliation of rival British, French and Belgian imperialist impulses. At the core of the real British motives for expansion in Africa were strategic, imperial and economic reasons.

---

[64] "Extract from monthly report for June 1917 by District Political Officer, Mwanza," FO 371/25857, PRO.

[65] "Allegations by Swede as to conduct of Belgian Colonial troops in E. Africa," October 18, 1917, FO 371/2857, PRO.

African interests simply provided British policy makers with a publicly acceptable explanation for new imperialist acquisitions, which happily coincided with their own self-image as peerless colonial administrators. British officials familiar with the intricacies of the issue, however, realized the glaring weakness of the public position: when African wishes differed from British priorities, they were disregarded.

Belgian Colonial Aims: Old Anxieties and Anticipated Acquisitions

Belgian decision makers, guiding a small state in an exposed geographical position, often had been nervous about the intentions of their more powerful neighbors during the early twentieth century. Belgian diplomats had reason for similar concern over the Belgian Congo. The Sangha and Lobaye corridors, which France had ceded to Germany in 1911, pointed directly at the Belgian Congo, which had become the only obstacle separating Cameroon and German East Africa. European press speculation over a possible repartition of central Africa by Germany and Britain heightened the unease in Brussels during 1911 and 1912.[66]

Belgians also remained particularly sensitive to criticism of their colonial policies. As a result of the Berlin Conference in 1884-85, a number of international restrictions had been placed upon the colony. The abuses of the Leopoldian regime's brutal concessionary companies led to an international furor and

---

[66] Jonathan E. Helmreich, *Belgium and Europe: A Study in Small Power Diplomacy* (The Hague: Mouton, 1976), p. 178; Jacques Willequet, *Le Congo Belge et la weltpolitik* (Brussels: Université libre de Bruxelles, 1962), pp. 327-328 and his article "Anglo-German Rivalry in Belgian and Portuguese Africa?" in *Britain and Germany in Africa*, ed. Gifford and Louis, pp. 245-273; and S.J.S. Cookey, *Britain and the Congo Question, 1885-1913* (London: Longmans, Green and Co., 1968), pp. 283-284.

Belgian colonial annexation in 1908. Although the Belgians had adopted administrative reforms in the Congo, the issue plagued relations with Britain for years.[67]

During the war Belgians rejected with scorn British allegations of colonial misrule and deficient performance in the East African campaign. Instead, they maintained that they had abandoned the Belgian Congo's neutrality at the behest of Britain and France, and under attack from German forces in East Africa. In the subsequent campaign in East Africa, they viewed their colonial forces as having played a significant role which deserved both recognition and compensation.

From the war's outset, Belgian concern about their position in central Africa was evident. Certainly this care was reflected in their attempt to maintain the Congo's neutrality, as guaranteed under Article X of the Berlin Act of 1885. When it became necessary to abandon that neutrality, the Belgian diplomat Pierre Orts had proposed to his government that in exchange for the sacrifice Belgium would be making, it might be suitable "that France and England guarantee us the possession of the Congo at the Peace."[68]

The British and French were willing to accommodate this Belgian desire. On September 19, 1914, Britain's ambassador to Belgium, with his French colleague present and concurring, made an official commitment "to support Belgium in every way in securing the integrity of her colonial possessions."[69]

---

[67] Mary Elizabeth Thomas, "Anglo-Belgian Military Relations and the Congo Question, 1911-1913," *Journal of Modern History* 25 (June 1953):157-165. To place the central African issue in the broader context of the two nations' European relations, see Jonathan E. Helmreich, "Belgian Concern over Neutrality and British Intentions, 1906-1914," *Journal of Modern History* 36 (December 1964):419-427.

[68] "Neutralité du Congo," Aug. 14, 1914, Af 1/2, AMAE,B.

[69] Communication from F. H. Villiers to Baron van der Elst, Sept. 19, 1914, ibid.

If this formal assurance quieted some old Belgian anxieties, still the country's wartime diplomacy sought further guarantees that Belgian colonial rule of the Congo would not be sacrificed in a peace settlement. An example of this continuing concern is found in a conversation between Belgium's ambassador to London, Paul Hymans, and Foreign Secretary Grey in January 1916. After commenting on Belgium's participation in the fighting in Africa, Hymans exhorted, "We have the legitimate preoccupation of conserving intact our colonial patrimony, and we attach a great value to a guarantee in this regard." Happily, he was able to report to the Belgian government "the categoric declaration of Sir Edward Grey: We want Belgium to keep the Congo."[70]

On April 29, the Belgians received their desired additional great power guarantee in the form of a French declaration of support for maintaining the existing territorial status of the Belgian Congo and providing it with a special indemnity for damages suffered during the course of the war. The same day, the British ambassador and the Russian chargé d'affaires informed Beyens in writing of their adherence to the declaration.[71]

War in central Africa also presented new opportunities and posed new dangers. Reeling from reverses in Europe, the Belgians were glad to be of assistance to the French in Cameroon

---

[70] Hymans to Beyens, January 29, 1916, ibid. A week later, and still seeking to reinforce the extent of Belgium's attachment to the Congo, Hymans told British diplomat Arthur Nicolson, "Our colony is the fruit of an immense effort. Many Belgians have poured out their blood there. ... The King received it from his predecessor and has not ceased to look after its development, he legitimately wants to assure its preservation." Hymans to Beyens, February 7, 1916, ibid.

[71] Annex of Beyens letter to his ministers in London and Paris, April 30, 1916, ibid; see also Michael Francis Palo, "The Diplomacy of Belgian War Aims during the First World War" (Ph.D. dissertation: University of Illinois at Urbana-Champaign, 1977), pp. 520-523.

and the British in Northern Rhodesia. Given the long and exposed eastern frontier of the Congo, it is not surprising that Belgian colonial officials soon were urging a joint offensive with the British against German East Africa. Although logical from a strictly military point of view, a Colonial Ministry memorandum from October 1916 reveals multifarious motives for such an attack.

After arguing that a defensive strategy exposed the Congo to invasion, the memorandum turned to the internal effects of inaction. The position paper explained that among the Congo's European community, some residents from neutral countries held sentiments favorable to Germany. Since they were spread throughout the colony and in close contact with the people, it was likely that the African population was aware of the military reverses Belgium – "Bula Matari" – had suffered in Europe. As a result, "Our prestige could suffer from it, [and] in the colonies authority rests above all on prestige."[72]

Wartime imperialist calculations about European prestige in African eyes were not, of course, restricted to the Belgians; both British and French decision makers also took African opinion into account. Yet here the Belgians provided an ad-

---

[72] "Note sur la politique de guerre suivie au Congo par le gouvernement belge," Oct. 12, 1916, Af 1/2, AMAE,B. The appellation Bula Matari, which means "he who breaks rocks," was originally given to Henry Stanley for his accomplishment in circumventing the rapids on the lower Congo by opening the difficult overland passage to Kinshasa (then Leopoldville). Crawford Young writes that the term "came to convey the image of a force which crushes all resistance" and that "it was soon transferred to the state as an abstraction, or to its European representatives as impersonal agents of domination." Crawford Young and Thomas Turner, *The Rise and Decline of the Zairian State* (Madison: University of Wisconsin Press, 1985), pp. 30-31. Although the term was commonly used, in the above context it may have been purposely intended as a linguistic device to reinforce the importance of maintaining the prestige of colonial authorities among the Congo's African population.

ditional dimension to the issue. The prestige value of colonial military action now was extended beyond the conflict in Africa to compensate for setbacks in Europe.

According to the Colonial Ministry memorandum, the presence of inactive colonial troops in the Belgian Congo also could be dangerous. Memories of past mutinies were recalled.[73] Pierre van Zuylen explains that discontent spread among the idle soldiers who were poorly housed and fed. Van Zuylen further asserts that this dissatisfaction was not restricted to the Congolese troops. Their Belgian officers were anxious to avenge the suffering of their compatriots.[74]

For Belgian decision makers, like their counterparts in the great powers, the spread of the war to Africa also created new vistas of colonial expansion.[75] German East Africa was not the principal focus of these Belgian designs, but it became an important component in their imperialist visions.

The chief territorial priority of most Belgian colonialists was the acquisition of Portuguese possessions on Africa's west coast. An early Belgian proposal, drafted for the Ministry of Foreign Affairs at the outset of 1915, outlined the extent of this objective and how it might be accomplished. In Africa, it noted that the Belgian Congo was large enough and that "we do not desire to increase it. But we ought to obtain from

---

[73] "Note sur la politique de guerre suivie au Congo," Oct. 12, 1916, Af 1/2, AMAE,B.

[74] Baron Pierre van Zuylen, *L'Echiquier congolais* (Brussels: Charles Dessart, 1959), p. 433.

[75] My analysis differs from Jean Stengers's assertion: "The country [Belgium] did not dream of acquiring other people's possessions. The acquisition of Ruanda-Urundi, after World War I – not indeed as a colony but as a mandate from the League of Nations – was in no way the result of expansionist ambitions." Included as the conclusion to his chapter, "The Congo Free State and the Belgian Congo Before 1914," *Colonialism in Africa, 1870-1960*, 5 vols., ed. Gann and Duignan, 1:290.

Portugal *Cabinda and the southern bank of the Congo from Noki to the sea*"[emphasis in original].[76] Belgium's great power allies should be pressed to obtain this from Portugal in return for compensation in German Southwest Africa.

A later memorandum from the Ministry of Foreign Affairs elaborated on the arguments Belgium could advance in favor of extending the Congo's coastline. Seeking the same territories from Portugal as the earlier proposal, the new paper suggested compensating Portugal from either German Southwest or East Africa. British assistance was to be enlisted in this effort by pointing out the help the Congo had given to Rhodesia and by turning over Ruanda to Britain.[77]

The Belgian motive for acquiring these Portuguese colonial territories bore striking similarity to the French desire to gain greater access to the ocean for their possessions in the African interior. From a geographical viewpoint, the giant Belgian Congo appeared an anomaly; encompassing 905,365 square miles, it had a tiny coastline of only 25 miles.

The navigable portion of the Congo below the major port of Matadi served as the border with the Portuguese colony of Angola. The prospect of interference with shipping at the Congo's only port was a particular Belgian fear. Heightening this threat was the possibility that Portuguese rule in Angola might one day be replaced by that of a great power, especially Germany. "One easily imagines the consequences for the Belgian Congo: Germany once ruler of our colony's only outlet to the sea and holding our capital under its cannons, it would be the end of the political and economic autonomy of the Congo."[78]

---

[76] Note prepared for the Ministry of Foreign Affairs, February 25, 1915, Af 1/2, AMAE,B; see similar proposal of January 25, 1915, ibid.

[77] Extract from a memorandum classified in the dossier "Régime politique de la Belgique après la guerre," copy dated April 23, 1915, ibid.

[78] "Note sur la politique de guerre suivie au Congo," October 12, 1916, ibid.

The priority that the Belgians were to attach to this expansion of the Congo's Atlantic coastline did not mean, however, that it was the only area in which they sought to enlarge their African colony. The anticipation, and later the pursuit, of the Belgian offensive in German East Africa gave rise to territorial ambitions in that region, too.

On January 17, 1915, Governor General F.A. Fuchs of the Belgian Congo offered an expansive view of what Belgium might hope to gain in German East Africa. In a letter to the colonial minister, Jules Renkin, he indicated it would be desirable to acquire not only Ruanda and Urundi, but also a vast area stretching from the border of Uganda in the north, to Bismarckburg at the southern end of Lake Tanganyika, and as far east as Tabora. Although he acknowledged that the British Cape-to-Cairo railroad project would traverse this area, he argued that this "need not be considered an obstacle because the existence of this railroad would in no way require the political alienation of the terrain which it crossed."[79]

Remarkably pretentious and unrealistic, Fuchs's vision of Belgian colonial expansion in East Africa would find more moderate echoes as the campaign in German East Africa unfolded. Belgian hopes of beginning such an offensive in 1915, however, were not to be realized. In May, Belgian Minister Albert de Bassompierre traveled to London to discuss the issue. The British government replied at the end of June that after careful consideration they had decided that "no general offensive" could be undertaken for the present by their forces in East Africa due to Britain's current military commitments in Europe.[80]

---

[79] Fuchs to Renkin, January 17, 1915, ibid. Renkin forwarded the letter along with his own cover letter to the foreign minister on March 19, 1915. He advised that he did not share Fuchs's opinions and therefore was sending the letter only for the purpose of information.

[80] From the memorandum which accompanied letter from Villiers to Davignon, June 29, 1915, ibid.

Only when Smuts began his advance in the vicinity of Mount Kilimanjaro at the outset of 1916 were the Belgians able to take the offensive. Crossing the frontier in late April, the Belgian colonial troops occupied Ruanda and Urundi by the end of June. Then advancing simultaneously with the British offensive, they moved south and east, taking Ujiji and Tabora.

Differences soon arose over the administration of the areas of German East Africa occupied by the Belgian colonial forces. Ambassador Francis Villiers informed the Belgians on April 17, 1916, that Britain was "prepared to undertake the whole control and administration of occupied territory until the conclusion of the war."[81]

Renkin quickly rejected this proposal. He argued that territories under military occupation were administered by the state occupying them as a matter of universal practice. The British proposal would reduce the Belgians to a subordinate position, having a negative effect on military morale and Belgian prestige among Africans.[82]

Confronted with this determined opposition, the British conceded the issue to the Belgians, replying on May 23 that they "would not further press the proposal." Instead, they accepted the Belgian counteroffer that a senior British political officer be attached to the headquarters of the Belgian forces in East Africa.[83]

In the fall of 1916 a new point of contention arose over the administration of the town of Tabora. This confused and acrimonious dispute, which continued until February 1917, centered on the transfer of the town from Belgian to British control. The original Belgian goal had been to turn Tabora over to the British in exchange for British recognition of their gains

---

[81] "Note verbale," April 17, 1916, ibid.

[82] Renkin to Beyens, Annex, May 3, 1916, ibid.

[83] Renkin to Beyens, May 23, 1916, ibid.

elsewhere in East Africa.[84] The British insisted upon the transfer of the town while resisting any acknowledgement of Belgian claims.[85] Eventually the Belgians were forced to give way, but not before the issue had engendered bad feelings in both countries.[86]

From the beginning of the Belgian invasion, one of their objectives was to obtain a pledge which might be redeemed at future peace talks. This intention was evident in the detailed letter of instructions which Renkin sent on March 27, 1916, to General Tombeur, commander of Belgian colonial troops in the Congo. "One of the aims of our military effort in Africa is, as you know, to assure our possession of a German territory as a pawn." The territory was not, however, to be acquired only for the purpose of bargaining. "If, at the moment when peace negotiations begin, modifications in the current territorial status of Africa are considered, the retention of this pawn would favor Belgian interests from all points of view," Renkin continued.[87]

Here is evidence of the developing Belgian program of colonial expansion on both the Congo's western and eastern frontiers. The acquisition of these territories was to become closely interrelated with the additional prospect that Belgian conquests in East Africa could be used as bargaining chips in peace negotiations.

The second part of a confidential memorandum delivered to British Ambassador Villiers on October 10, 1916, sets forth Belgian territorial aspirations in Africa. It describes the area conquered by Belgium in East Africa as "one of the best parts

[84] Louis, *Ruanda-Urundi 1884-1919*, pp. 225-227.

[85] Villiers to Beyens, November 10, 1916; Villiers to Beyens, November 29, 1916; Villiers to Beyens, January 17, 1917, Af 1/2, AMAE,B.

[86] See record of Orts conversation with Villiers on October 28, 1916; and Renkin to Beyens, January 27, 1917, ibid.

[87] Renkin to Tombeur, March 27, 1915, ibid; see also Louis, *Ruanda-Urundi 1884-1919*, p. 216.

of the German colony." Valuable because it provided Belgian access to Lake Victoria and control over part of the German central railway, the region also contained "lands such as Ruanda, fertile, rich in cattle and suitable for white settlement."[88]

The specific objectives which Belgian policy makers would seek in return for their conquest were as yet undecided. The British were informed that "Belgium has not yet taken a decision on the question of whether or not it is desirable to conserve the conquered territories." Yet the memorandum explained the basis upon which such a decision would be reached:

> If Belgium can obtain, by the retrocession of all or part of the conquered territory, a political or economic advantage in Europe or in Africa, of a value equal to that of the territory, the interest of Belgium will probably lead the royal government to abandon its conquest to obtain this advantage. The Belgian point of view is simple: it intends to derive from the considerable military effort it has expended in Africa the greatest possible advantage. If it can gain a greater advantage by ceding back its conquest, it will cede back its conquest.[89]

Thus, the Belgians sought to keep their options open, hoping to gain the most beneficial return for their East African conquests. In spite of this intention, they were willing to state their territorial desiderata for the Belgian Congo. It was, they argued, a modest territorial acquisition: "Cabinda and the Portuguese province of the left bank of the Bas-Congo." The report continued, "This desire is legitimate, since it is of considerable interest for the power which controls almost the complete physical basin of the Congo to possess the course of the river to the sea."[90]

---

[88] Note en 3 parties, October 10, 1916, Af 1/2, AMAE,B.

[89] Ibid.

[90] Ibid.

The report suggested that the envisioned concessions be made whether Belgium dealt with Germany or another power. Other Belgian colonial interests mentioned in the note include an indemnity and retaining territory in East Africa; most favorable tariffs on the central railway to Dar es Salaam; and a revision of the Berlin Act.

A month later, the British replied with a diplomatic but forthright refusal to acknowledge the Belgian colonial claims. Communicating a telegram from Foreign Secretary Grey, Villiers pressed Belgian Foreign Minister Beyens on the provisional nature of all territorial occupation until the end of the war. Although the Belgian notes accepted this, Villiers continued:

> ... it would seem that the Belgian Government take the view that in the final peace negotiations they can make separate arrangements with Germany as to [the] future of territory occupied by them, as though it was definitely in their possession. His Majesty's Government could not agree in advance to such a position, which has not been claimed for themselves or for any of the allies.[91]

This British response failed to move Colonial Minister Renkin. Informed of the British position, he dismissed its objections as unwarranted and upheld the justice of Belgium's claims. Britain knew perfectly well that Belgium would not conclude a separate arrangement with Germany. "In affecting to suppose the opposite intention, it is turning to a simple artifice of discussion," he stated.[92]

Despite Britain's reservations, Renkin argued that Belgium had participated in the war in Africa and because of this would be entitled to participate in the peace negotiations. "The desire of Belgium to enter into possession of the left bank of the Congo

---

[91] Villiers to Beyens, November 10, 1916, Af 1/2, AMAE,B.

[92] Renkin to Beyens, November 28, 1916, ibid.

is so legitimate, and our conquests facilitate its realization, that I cannot think England is hostile in principle to it."[93]

This commitment to territorial aggrandizement in Africa would remain Belgian policy until the partition of Germany's colonies at the peace conference. The extension of the Congo's Atlantic coast continued to be the foremost concern of Belgian imperialists, but the prospect of retaining Ruanda, Urundi and possibly additional territory in East Africa proved increasingly attractive.

The lesson of the fall of 1916 was that Belgium, without abandoning any of its colonial ambitions, would have to wait for the proper opportunity to gain British acquiescence. Paul Hymans, still Belgium's ambassador to Britain, demonstrated this attitude in a discussion with Lord Robert Cecil almost a year later. "Belgium has aspirations in Africa," he explained. "They have been stated by the Belgian government in a note of October 10, 1916. Our policy is moderate and reasonable." Nevertheless, he acknowledged, "This is not the moment to discuss them."[94]

Before the right moment would arrive at the Paris Peace Conference, another perceived threat to Belgian colonial rule in Africa would arise. The proposal of the British Labour Party for the internationalization of central Africa seemed to threaten not only the colonial gains Belgium hoped to make, but perhaps even Belgian possession of the Congo.[95]

---

[93] Ibid.

[94] Hymans to Foreign Minister de Broqueville, September 7, 1917, ibid.

[95] This idea was included in the Labour Party memorandum of December 1917, which stated the Party's war aims. The following February the position was altered to allow the colonial states to retain their administrative powers. See Partha Gupta, *Imperialism and the British Labour Movement, 1914-1964* (New York: Homes and Meier Publishers, 1975), p. 51.

Belgium's ambassadors in London and Paris repeatedly stated their opposition to international control. In January 1918, Belgium's minister to London, Baron Ludovic Moncheur, told Lord Robert Cecil that Labour's plan "of entrusting all of tropical Africa to an international organization, naturally was not of a kind that would appeal to us." Cecil responded that the idea was impractical, and the Belgians should not take the proposition seriously.[96]

In spite of this assurance, Belgian opposition to internationalization was restated by Renkin when he visited Lloyd George later that month. Moncheur writes that Renkin informed Lloyd George of "what a painful impression a similar proposition would make in Belgium, where all the citizens now considered their colony as an intrinsic part of the nation." Lloyd George's reply, like Cecil's, seemed designed to ease Belgian concern. He pointed out that the proposal was "far from being shared by a majority of the Labour Party." In addition, he described international administration as detestable, recalling that in Egypt it almost had led to war between Britain and France.[97] Yet as reassuring as this may have seemed, Moncheur would report the following month that the British cabinet would not be "disposed to strongly support the objections which we could make to the imposition of an international administration in Africa, if their own territories can escape it."[98]

Given these continuing doubts about Britain, the news from Paris must have been a welcome antidote. Belgian Ambassador de Gaiffier reported on February 7, 1918, a conversation he had with Pierre de Margerie of the French Foreign Ministry. De Margerie, who would become French ambassador to Belgium in 1919, had told him that very shortly the British

---

[96] Moncheur to Hymans, January 4, 1918, Af 1/2, AMAE,B. Hymans replaced de Broqueville as foreign minister in January 1918.

[97] Moncheur to Hymans, January 26, 1918, ibid.

[98] Moncheur to Hymans, February 27, 1918, ibid.

would be informed of the determined French opposition to the internationalization of tropical Africa. "In this question, as in so many others," de Margerie continued, "our interests coincide with yours, and you can be absolutely sure of us."[99]

Thus Belgium, like its great power allies, found its colonial aims challenged by the new political attitudes developing in the last years of the war. In many ways, Belgium's wartime policies of imperialist expansion in Africa had proved as ambitious as those of its more powerful neighbors. Where they differed most clearly was in the particular fear and concern of Belgian decision makers, common enough among small states, that their nation's interests might be disregarded.

---

[99] De Gaiffier to Hymans, February 7, 1918, ibid.

4

The Armistice:
Colonies or Mandates?

The tide of battle having clearly turned in favor of the
Allies, Germany's new chancellor, Prince Max von Baden, appealed on October 4, 1918, for an armistice and a peace settlement based on President Wilson's Fourteen Points. Although
the armistice would not come for more than a month, the inter-
Allied exchanges which followed Prince Max's request began
the process of converting Allied wartime aims into concrete
objectives to be obtained at the peace conference.

The long-developing British, French and Belgian desires
for colonial expansion did not abate in late 1918. Opposition to returning Germany's colonies remained nearly universal among the leaders of the Allied states. Officials concerned
with colonial affairs employed the months preceding the peace
conference to justify the extensive acquisitions they coveted.
In Africa, each Allied state endeavored at least to hold on to
the territories its forces had occupied during the war.

In both the United States and Britain, elections in late
1918 indicated popular support for a vindictive peace with
Germany. Arno Mayer has pointed out that these electoral results produced determined right-wing pressures on both Wilson and Lloyd George.[1] Still the repeated proclamations of

---

[1] Arno J. Mayer, *Politics and Diplomacy of Peacemaking: Contain-
ment and Counterrevolution at Versailles, 1918-1919* (New York: Alfred
A. Knopf, 1967), p. 119.

anti-imperialist war aims since 1917 had created a strong public impression. Even in the flush of victory, Western European leaders thought it necessary to provide an altruistic public cloak for their conquests.

Complicating this situation further was the position of President Wilson. His authority had been undercut by the Republican victory in the November elections, and European leaders were aware of this fact. Yet he continued to command considerable political and moral strength while genuinely sharing many of the popular anti-imperialist attitudes.

In these circumstances, the preparations for the peace conference represent a significant juncture. Proponents of contending colonial settlements intensified efforts to justify their positions and achieve their aims while seeking to maintain an apparent public accord.

Contending Components of British Policy

The potential for conflict was foreshadowed in the pre-armistice deliberations of the British government. During October, President Wilson and the German government exchanged a succession of notes concerning the conditions Germany would have to accept before an armistice would be granted. Knowledge of these discussions engendered debate in Western European capitals over whether they should accept Wilson's terms or attach their own reservations to any armistice agreement.

In Britain, the principal concern was to ensure that if the armistice was granted on Wilson's terms, his vague declarations on freedom of the seas would not prove detrimental to British naval security. Colonial questions, however, were also considered. Of Wilson's Fourteen Points, Point Five's demand for "A free, open-minded, and absolutely impartial adjustment of all colonial claims" could have posed a threat to the annexation of Germany's colonies by Britain and the Dominions.

British insistence on retaining Germany's colonies was re-iterated at the War Cabinet's afternoon session of October 14. Foreign Secretary Balfour, in a succinct comment, stated that Britain was "bound" to ensure that Germany's colonies in the Pacific and Southwest Africa were allocated to the appropriate southern Dominions.

Focusing on Africa, Lloyd George sought to establish a politically palatable justification for British annexation. He inquired of General Smuts "whether it would be possible to summon a small Indaba [Conference or Parley] of Native Chiefs in the ex-German colonies in Africa, which could be put in as evidence at the Peace Conference, with regard to the wishes of the native inhabitants." Smuts responded that considerable testimony of this sort, which confirmed opposition to restoring any of Germany's colonies, had already been collected.[2]

Yet the extent to which British policy makers might draw favorable conclusions from this material was questioned by Lord Robert Cecil, now assistant secretary of state for foreign affairs. He asserted that "while undoubtedly a great case had been made out against the return of the colonies to Germany, it was not so easy to make out the case for our keeping them."[3]

Perhaps this argument influenced the prime minister, for he queried the War Cabinet about suggesting that the United States send officers to the former German colonies who could report directly to President Wilson. Replying with caution, Balfour observed that "such a course might be desirable if they could ensure the selection of officers who were both impartial and competent. This would not be easy."[4]

Given its context, the logical inference to be drawn from Balfour's remark is that it would be necessary, as well as diffi-cult, to find American officers sympathetic to British colonial

---

[2] War Cabinet Minutes, October 14, 1918, CAB 23/8, PRO.

[3] Ibid.

[4] Ibid.

aims. In a sense, this comment reflects the general tone of the discussion. Those present were concerned primarily with how "to make out the case" for retaining the German colonies.

A memorandum circulated the following day by Colonial Secretary Walter Long provides a significant illustration of the way evidence for these territorial claims was being developed. In a cover note referring to the cabinet's discussion, Long described the memorandum as a sketch of the "steps which have already been taken to ascertain the feelings of the natives in the ex-German Colonies with regard to their remaining under British Rule."[5]

The first document in the memorandum is a secret telegram sent by Long to the southern Dominions on January 4, 1918, in which he informed them of British views and requested appropriate supporting evidence.

> It is the firm conviction of His Majesty's Government that, for security of Empire after the War, it is necessary to retain possession of German Colonies, but it has not been possible to secure general acceptance of this view owing to divergence of opinion among Allies. Great stress was laid by Russians during recent negotiations with Germans on right of population of country to determine its future, and proposal was made to apply this to German Colonies. There are indications in French newspapers, for instance, that this line of argument will be pressed in other quarters. I should, therefore, be glad if I could be furnished with a statement suitable for publication, if necessary, containing evidence of anxiety of natives

---

[5] Colonial Office, "German Colonies. Attitude of natives towards remaining under British Rule," G.T. 5994, 15/10/1918, CAB 24/66, PRO.

of (German New Guinea) (Samoa) (South-West Africa) to live under British rule.[6]

Certainly a revealing telegram, it offers an unusually candid insight into British motives for seeking the opinions of the German colonies' inhabitants. As might be expected, the responses to the telegram portrayed a widespread desire for British administration.

In several places, however, the competence of the German colonies' inhabitants to participate in decisions about their future was questioned seriously. This particularly was true of German East Africa (Long's memorandum stated that a telegram similar to the one quoted above had been sent to British administrators in East and West Africa on January 8). As elsewhere, German colonial rule in East Africa was criticized as brutal. Yet it was alleged that due to the hardships of the war, it would not be prudent to poll the population.

The administrator was quite opposed to the principle of a plebiscite but, given twelve months of peaceful administration, he had not the slightest doubt that the mass of people, as opposed to the ex-German minor officials, would infinitely prefer to remain under the protection of the British.[7]

Long's memorandum solicited evidence that Africans in the German colonies favored British rule, and not surprisingly the colonial secretary had been told that this was the case. Yet the nature of the request and the ambiguity in the response from East Africa both suggest that the rationale of African preferences was regarded more as a foregone conclusion justifying British annexation than as a principle open to impartial examination.

Such an appraisal of colonial office motives is reinforced by the position paper Long circulated in October 1918. It listed

---

[6] Ibid.
[7] Ibid.

African interests as only one among several determinants compelling British acquisition of the German colonies. Initially the paper presents three general considerations which applied to all of the German colonies. First, the British Empire's security rested upon "the security of its ocean routes." Should the German submarine menace spread throughout the world's oceans, it would pose a deadly threat. Second, evidence that the Germans would build up a "strong native army" would force corresponding preparations throughout the British Empire. Finally, "the natives themselves wherever they have been articulate desire our rule."[8]

The "danger of a large native army" being raised by the Germans was portrayed as especially acute in East Africa. The long and difficult military campaign was evidence of the future trouble such an army might create. Further grounds for British retention of the colony could be found in its fine harbors on the "hitherto peaceable Indian Ocean." In addition, public opinion in the Union of South Africa and India supported keeping the colony.[9]

In conclusion, Long argued that the British Empire and Commonwealth should retain all of the German colonies except those in which they recognized French and Japanese claims. Condominium proposals were rejected as unworkable, as were any new ideas about internationalization. Justification, continued the self-confident voice of the Colonial Office, could be found in the interests of the inhabitants of the German colonies: "We need not fear to appeal to experience in claiming boldly that no type of government could be set up in countries like the tropical German Colonies which would work better than

---

[8] Imperial War Cabinet, "Our Desiderata in Regard to the Disposal of Territory taken from the Enemy," Colonial Office, October 1918, CAB 29/2/66969, PRO.

[9] Ibid.

British administration, and that British administration is in the direct interest of the natives."[10]

Long's views reveal the continued cogency in late 1918 of earlier wartime motives for British colonial expansion. In East Africa, strategic concerns remained prominent. They had been exacerbated by the wartime activity of submarines and the determined resistance of German colonial troops. At the same time, Long's defense of British colonial policy responded to concern for African interests in Britain and the United States.[11]

As his opinions indicate, the colonial secretary was among the most zealous British proponents of annexing Germany's colonies, but to some extent most other British and imperial leaders shared his attitudes. Balfour's comment of October 14 had affirmed that the interests of South Africa, Australia and New Zealand must be the crucial elements in determining the policy of the British Empire toward German Southwest Africa and the South Pacific.

Dominion voices were not limited strictly to these colonies. Prime Ministers William Hughes of Australia and William Massey of New Zealand, along with Louis Botha and Smuts of South Africa, were intransigent opponents of returning Germany's former possessions and determined defenders of British colonial expansion.[12] Smuts had been at the forefront of the

---

[10] Ibid.

[11] More evidence of his attitude is to be found in "Africa. Natives of tropical Africa, welfare of," Memorandum by Mr. W. Long, December 18, 1918, G.T. 6518, CAB 24/72, PRO. There he notes that the question of native welfare in tropical Africa will be discussed at the peace conference and that "the American representatives will show considerable interest" in it. He argues that Britain consistently has been in the forefront of states attempting to enforce the Brussels Act of 1890 in regard to arms and liquor traffic and should take the initiative in proposing its extension.

[12] For example, in his letter to Lloyd George on September 2, 1918,

public alarm raised over the military danger a German *Mittelafrika* would pose to the British Empire.[13]

White South African leaders considered using German East Africa for their own purposes. Delagoa Bay had long been an Afrikaner territorial objective because it would have improved the Transvaal's access to the sea. Proposals within the South African government envisioned a territorial exchange that would give the Union of South Africa southern Mozambique and compensate Portugal with the southeastern part of German East Africa.[14]

From South Africa there also came a reasoned objection to the direction the repartition of the continent appeared to be taking at the end of the war. The South African Native National Congress, which later became the African National Congress, addressed a memorial to the British king on December 16, 1918. In large part, the document recounted the loyalty the black population had shown to the British government, requesting in return that London intervene to lessen their oppression and see that voting rights were extended to the African population.

With regard to the former German colonies, the petition urged that the African populations be consulted before any decisions were made. The harsh discrimination they suffered in the Union of South Africa influenced their advice to the British government on the redistribution of the German colonies. Point Eleven of the memorial argued, "That both German South-

---

Massey had declared, "I am utterly opposed to handing over any of the German Colonies or Palestine to the United States either in trust or in any other way." Lloyd George Papers, F/36/4/3, HLRO.

[13] Louis, *Great Britain and Germany's Lost Colonies*, pp. 101-102.

[14] See Ronald Hyam, *The Failure of South African Expansion, 1908-1948* (London: Macmillan, 1972), pp. 28-33 and P.R. Warhurst, "Smuts and Africa: a study in sub-imperialism," *South African Historical Journal* 16 (1984):84-87.

West and German South-East [Africa] should never be handed to the Union Government of South Africa unless its system of rule be radically altered so as to dispel colour prejudice."[15]

Further, the memorial suggested that a propitious moment had arrived to dislodge the Belgians from the Congo because of their misrule of the territory. To present its views, the Congress also sent a deputation to London and Versailles.[16]

These proposals by black South Africans for colonial adjustments, as well as their hopes for internal reforms, were ignored by Lloyd George's government. Repeatedly, London referred the questions back to Pretoria, claiming it could not interfere in the internal affairs of a self-governing Dominion.

Officials in South Africa replied with the expected rejection of internal criticism and a dismissal of the African proposals for the German colonies. "The destinies of the late German Colonial possessions in Africa referred to in the Memorial are in the hands of the Peace Conference, and fall for decision by the combined wisdom of the Statesmen of the Allied Powers,"[17] observed the secretary for native affairs. South African preferences were to influence the colonial peace settlement, but they were to represent only the views of the white minority.

---

[15] "Memorial to His Most Gracious Majesty King George V," by order of the South African Native National Congress, S.M. Makgatho, President; I. Bud-Mbelle, General Secretary, December 16, 1918, F/227/2, Lloyd George Papers, HLRO.

[16] Peter Walshe, *The Rise of African Nationalism in South Africa: The African National Congress 1912-1952* (Berkeley and Los Angeles: University of California Press, 1971), pp. 62-65 and Edward Roux, *Time Longer than Rope*, 2d ed. (Madison: University of Wisconsin Press, 1964), pp. 110-111.

[17] E. Barrett, Secretary for Native Affairs, Reply to the "Memorial from South African Native National Congress," Pretoria, July 28, 1919, F/227/2, Lloyd George Papers, HLRO.

The India Office, too, took a direct interest in German East Africa during the latter part of 1918.[18] Seeking to promote and protect what they perceived to be Indian self-esteem and welfare, India's British representatives proposed that the former German colony become an Indian colony or mandate or at least a site for Indian colonization. In this advocacy role, the India Office generally encountered a skeptical reception and found itself in conflict with the aims of the Colonial Office, which frequently took the part of the European settlers in East Africa.

An example of the Anglo-Indian position is found in a strong plea by the secretary of state for India, Edwin S. Montagu, for granting special consideration to Indian immigration into German East Africa. He accepted that nothing should be done which would be prejudicial to African interests, but he sought to refute arguments by Long and Curzon that Indian immigration would be incompatible with this principle. Instead, he upheld the justification offered in an earlier memorandum by Sir Theodore Morison that Indian civilization was "far more easily comprehensible" to Africans than European civilization.[19]

Indians, Montagu maintained, might be assigned to uninhabited areas, where they could work as small farmers. This he compared favorably with the European plantation system. Under the Germans, Africans had been forced to labor on European estates. Although the British relied instead upon "moral persuasion," Montagu observed: "How this is applied I cannot say, but all accounts agree that the native is an unwilling labourer, but yet the White Man's farms are cultivated."[20]

---

[18] For a complete discussion of this interest see Herbert Lüthy, "India and East Africa: Imperial Partnership at the End of the First World War," *Journal of Contemporary History* 6 (1971):55-85.

[19] Edwin S. Montagu, "India and German East Africa," November 28, 1918, G.T. 6407, CAB 24/71/67062, PRO.

[20] Ibid. John Overton's article, "War and Economic Development: Settlers in Kenya, 1914-1918," *Journal of African History* 27 (1986):79-103,

Montagu did not press for German East Africa as an Indian colony but insisted that some provision for Indian colonization was the only equitable solution.

> But if we do not do this at least, I am afraid there will be many who might argue: "Is not the cruelty of the German towards the native population, is not the danger of submarine bases, a new form of the old sanitation dodge [a specious argument used to separate Indian and European communities in East Africa]? ... The South African wants to keep German South-West Africa, and the East African trader wants the rich lands of German East Africa. Under various disguises and pretexts this is our real motive for annexation. Because India cannot speak with the same authority, ... she cannot obtain in any of the new territories conditions comparable to those that are going to be given to sons of the Empire of European descent."[21]

The secretary of state for India carefully pointed out that he did not agree with such an analysis. Yet if India received nothing, British arguments in favor of retaining German East Africa would appear to many people as simply excuses used to support the territorial avarice of British settlers in East Africa. By raising this line of reasoning, Montagu intimates

---

forcefully argues that the wartime conditions produced prosperity and expansion in the settler economy of Kenya. He also provides an answer for the war years to Montagu's observation. Africans seeking to avoid harsh service in the carrier corps provided a steady labor supply (pp. 88-89).

[21] Montagu, "India and German East Africa." See also "Memorandum on German East Africa by Sir S.P. Sinha, K.C.," December 20, 1918, G.T. 6520, CAB 24/72, PRO. Sinha, while recognizing the priority of native rights, sees a "civilising mission" for India. He concludes, "India alone of the Empire, would appear to be about to receive directly nothing as a result of the war."

the sensitivity of British decision makers to criticism of their motives.

The strength of expansionist attitudes within the British government's inner circles had the potential to threaten harmonious relations with Washington. Foreign perception of the strong British opposition to a return of the German colonies is found in a letter from the Belgian ambassador to Paris, de Gaiffier, to Belgian Foreign Minister Hymans. Reporting on an Allied meeting at which he sat next to Lord Alfred Milner, de Gaiffier described the British position on the German colonies. Milner had portrayed Britain as a satisfied colonial power, while stating the southern Dominions' interests in their respective areas. Yet, the British delegate continued, "if President Wilson..., interpreted the article of his program relative to the colonies in the sense of their restitution to Germany, he would have to send his fleet and a million men against us, against the South Africans, against the Australians."[22]

Despite the strength of such sentiments in favor of territorial acquisitions, there were important advocates of a conciliatory accord with the United States.[23] Many British decision makers, such as the prime minister, were determined to achieve both ends. Lloyd George, while supporting the substance of the Dominions' claims, worked to prevent colonial questions from disrupting Anglo-American relations. In accordance with this approach, he was willing to explore the idea of the United States becoming a trustee for one of the German colonies.

---

[22] De Gaiffier to Hymans, October 25, 1918, "Entretien avec Lord Milner sur le sort des Colonies," Af 1/2 8633, AMAE,B.

[23] William Roger Louis, "Great Britain and the African Peace Settlement of 1919," *American Historical Review* 71 (April-July 1966):877. According to the author, these included not only the British prime minister but also Prime Minister Borden of Canada, General Smuts and Lord Milner.

On October 29, Lloyd George spoke privately with Colonel
Edward House, who was representing President Wilson in pre-
armistice discussions with the Allies. According to House, he
was told that because of inhuman German colonial policies,
"Great Britain was unwilling" to permit the return of the
German colonies and that the southern Dominions must receive their respective shares of the German colonies or "Great
Britain would be confronted by a revolution in those dominions."[24]

At the same time, the prime minister made a diplomatic
proposal which, in light of the wartime interest Britain had developed in retaining German East Africa, must appear startling.
Lloyd George told House that Great Britain wanted "the United
States to become trustee for German East African colonies."
In the colonel's opinion, however, the aim of the "suggestion
regarding German East Africa, is that the British would like
us to accept something so they might more freely take what
they desire."[25]

Later, Lloyd George wrote of the proposition that it was
a suggestion he had "thrown out" to House, and that House
had shown no interest in it.[26] In the same place, the prime
minister described all the British ministers, with the exception
of Long, as reluctant to increase Britain's colonies. He argued
that the policies adopted toward Germany's colonies resulted
from the positions of the Dominions and the possible military
repercussions of returning the colonies to Germany.[27]

---

[24] House to Lansing, October 30, 1918, *Foreign Relations of the United
States*, 1918, Supplement I, pp. 421-423, quoted in Harry Rudin, *Armistice
1918* (New Haven: Yale University Press, 1944; reprint ed., Hamden, Conn.:
Archon Books, 1967), p. 270.

[25] Ibid.

[26] Lloyd George, *The Truth about the Peace Treaties*, 2 vols. (London:
Victor Gollancz, 1938), 1:115.

[27] Ibid., pp. 115-131.

The most convincing explanation for this apparent lapse into anti-imperialism is that the British government placed a high priority on good Anglo-American relations during the uncertainties of late 1918. Discussion in the Imperial War Cabinet suggested that this was the case, while indicating British awareness that despite their willingness to make concessions none would be required.

Curzon observed that the United States might not be interested in colonial obligations and, if it were, Africa might not be the preferable location. "Mr. Lloyd George agreed that this was probable, but that by making the offer to America we would remove any prejudice against us on the ground of 'land-grabbing.'"[28]

Smuts, however, raised objections to surrendering German East Africa.

> The British Empire was the great African Power right along the eastern half of the continent, and securing East Africa would give us through communication along the whole length of the continent... In his opinion it was not only on the grounds of our conquests and sacrifices, but on the obvious geographical situation, that we were entitled to make a strong claim of being the mandatory in that region. Personally he would give up very much in order to attain that. He was not putting in a claim to East Africa for the South African Union, but the view he had expressed would be very strongly felt in the Union, which had taken the main share in the conquest of East Africa. He would prefer to see the United States in Palestine rather than East Africa.[29]

---

[28] Ibid., p. 118.
[29] Ibid., pp. 119-120.

The exchange of views at this December meeting of the Imperial War Cabinet continued without arriving at a concrete position on the future of the German colonies in tropical Africa. By the end of 1918, significant voices from the British Empire had been raised for retaining German East Africa, but this remained a collateral British objective. Other colonial territories were of more importance, as were good relations with the United States.

Draft resolutions on the captured German colonies which Sir Maurice Hankey, secretary of the Imperial War Cabinet, submitted to Lloyd George on December 21, 1918, illustrate these positions. In his cover letter, he noted that Prime Ministers Borden of Canada and Botha of South Africa, along with Hughes and Balfour, had been consulted. Concerning the German colonies coveted by South Africa, Australia and New Zealand, Hankey proposed that "the Imperial War Cabinet give their strong and unqualified support to the claim for their incorporation with these Dominions."[30]

For the other German colonies and Turkish territories, mandates were recommended. Following a description of the conditions under which the mandates were to be established, Hankey suggested that "one of the first steps should be to ascertain whether President Wilson accepts the above principles, and whether the United States of America are prepared to become one of the mandatory Powers." The draft proposal continued,

> Pending an expression of the views of President Wilson on these questions, it would be premature to reach any final conclusions as to the scheme for the administration by the various possible mandatory Powers of the territories con-

---

[30] Hankey to Lloyd George, "Preliminary Draft of Conclusions of the Imperial War Cabinet, The Disposal of the Captured German Colonies and Turkish Territories," December 21, 1918, Lloyd George Papers, F/23/3/31, HLRO.

cerned. The Imperial War Cabinet consider, however, that there is a very strong case for the assumption of this responsibility by the British Commonwealth in the case of Mesopotamia, Arabia,
Palestine and German East Africa.[31]

A telling marginal comment – implying East Africa's low
priority – notes, "in the following order of importance." Even
more clearly, the memorandum indicates that the British viewed
American attitudes as crucial in determining the future of the
captured German colonies. Yet as late as December 1918, the
American position on the likely postwar colonial redistribution
remained imprecise, particularly with regard to tropical Africa.

The United States and the Evolution of the Mandate Concept

This indeterminate American position did not mean no attempt had been made to formulate new colonial initiatives.
Colonel House, under instructions from President Wilson, had
organized a group of experts to prepare for the peace conference in September 1917. The work of this body, known as
the Inquiry, was at first slow. Finding a group of American
scholars who were experts on Africa proved impossible.[32] Yet
eventually a prodigious amount of background material was
collected, the African division gathering fifty-four reports on a
wide variety of topics.[33]

The man who emerged as the chief American expert on
Africa was the historian George Louis Beer. Beer's field of

---

[31] Ibid.

[32] Lawrence E. Gelfand, *The Inquiry: American Preparations for Peace,
1917-1919* (New Haven: Yale University Press, 1963), p. 227 and Arthur
Walworth, *America's Moment, 1918: American Diplomacy at the End of
World War I* (New York: W.W. Norton and Co., 1977), p. 77.

[33] Gelfand, p. 228.

specialization had been British colonial commerce during the seventeenth and eighteenth centuries. In late 1917, he turned his energy toward contemporary colonial problems and began his work for the Inquiry.

Shortly thereafter Beer made a proposal which would bear a striking resemblance to the mandate system devised for central Africa in 1919. Describing in broad terms what the characteristics of this program should be, he suggested the incorporation of international guarantees for native rights and economic free trade. Writing to the Inquiry's director, Sidney Mezes, on December 31, 1917, Beer opposed internationalization but observed:

> In case of any transfer of territory in Central Africa, and possibly even in the existing dependencies, it might, I think be definitely established, that the state exercising sovereignty in Africa is proceeding under an international mandate and must act as trustee primarily for the nations and secondarily for the outside world as a whole.[34]

Lawrence Gelfand joins earlier writers in acknowledging that Beer, in this and other proposals at the beginning of 1918, may have been the first to use the term "mandate" in the form later accepted at the peace conference.[35] In the detailed

---

[34] Beer to Sidney Mezes, December 31, 1917, Mezes MSS, Columbia University Library, quoted by Gelfand, pp. 231-2.

[35] Ibid. In giving Beer credit for the term, James Shotwell refers to a Beer memorandum of January 1, 1918, on Mesopotamia in "The Paris Peace Conference," *George Louis Beer: A Tribute to His Life and Work in the Making of History and the Moulding of Public Opinion* (New York: Macmillan Co., 1924), p. 86. See also Louis Gray, editor's preface to Beer, *African Questions at the Paris Peace Conference* (New York: Macmillan Co., 1923) p. xix and Ingram Bandar, "Sidney E. Mezes and the Inquiry," *Journal of Modern History* 11 (1939):201.

reports which he prepared for the Inquiry during 1918, Beer also advanced more specific propositions on colonial questions.

In a report on the German colonies in Africa, written for the Inquiry in February 1918, Beer recognized that "political expediency" most likely would be the dominant force in determining their future. Still, he believed it was important to study the question impartially. German misrule before the war negated the possibility of returning the colonies. Instead, for German East Africa, he suggested that "thorough consideration" be given to a project for Indian immigration.

In West Africa, Beer attacked the prewar boundaries as artificial. He readily conceded France's right to a return of those parts of Cameroon which Germany had received in 1911. For the remainder of Cameroon, he mentioned the possibilities of American trusteeship and internationalization. He surmised, however, that "neither proposal appears to be feasible. In that event, possibly the only solution is to assign part of the Cameroons to British Nigeria and part to French Equatorial Africa."[36]

By the end of October, Beer had added to these suggestions a detailed historical analysis of modern efforts to establish international control in tropical Africa. Beginning with the Berlin Conference of 1884-85, he described the steps taken to regulate trade, liquor and arms, along with such other topics as native rights and militarization. Beer perceived progress but stated that more must be done to avoid sacrificing African interests to those of the European states.

---

[36] Beer, "The German Colonies in Africa," written for the Inquiry, February 12-26, 1918, in *African Questions at the Paris Peace Conference*, pp. 57-67. Beer's willingness to agree to such a partition was predicated upon the acceptance of international control by the mandatory powers. This was to include the protection of native rights and an economic guarantee of the "open door," in which case, "it matters comparatively little to the world at large which flag flies in the Cameroons." p. 67.

The future neutralization of tropical Africa was rejected; instead, Beer hoped that the League of Nations would prevent future wars. "Provided the welfare of the African aborigines be fully considered, it is not unjustifiable to wage such wars in Africa," he observed. "But it is ignoble to use Africa merely as a pawn to purchase security elsewhere at the expense of the native."[37]

Despite this semblance of altruism, Beer recognized that certain interests of Washington's allies would require accommodation. French wartime recruitment in Africa meant that Paris was unlikely to agree to neutralization. The campaign in East Africa, and Germany's plans for a vast new colonial empire in central Africa, likewise were credited with creating great anxiety in South Africa. There, "any necessity of arming the natives would imperil the delicately balanced fabric."[38]

Here, and elsewhere in Beer's position papers, is evidence that his analysis of contemporary Africa was influenced heavily by the current thinking of Allied imperialists. This was particularly true with regard to those in the British Empire. Beer was, in fact, a member of the Round Table group. This association, inspired by Lord Milner, promoted British imperialism of the supposedly more enlightened form which included the active participation of the Commonwealth. By the end of 1918, members of the Round Table had "expanded their im-

---

[37] Beer, "Middle Africa: Problems of International Cooperation and Control," written for the Inquiry, completed October 31, 1918, in *African Questions at the Paris Peace Conference*, p. 266.

[38] Ibid., p. 275. An observation by Belgian analysts reveals that they shared this perception of South African attitudes. "General Smuts is very hostile to the militarization of blacks.... His preoccupation is not to arm the blacks, in order to conserve for the white race, in the Union of South Africa, supremacy over the black race." "Programme des revendications de la Belgique dans le domaine colonial," Première partie, Principes généraux, p. 57, Papiers Orts, 433, Archives générales du royaume, Brussels (AGR).

perial vision to include the United States in an Anglo-Saxon world mission."[39]

Beer's interaction with this group reveals both the historian's anglophile views and the transatlantic development of the mandate idea. The footnotes of Beer's position papers refer frequently to British colonialist journals, such as the *United Empire Magazine*, the *Geographical Journal* and the *Journal of the African Society*, as well as similar continental publications and government documents.

Ideas moved across the Atlantic in the opposite direction, too. For instance, William Roger Louis attributes partial credit to Beer for the article "Windows of Freedom."[40] The article, which appeared in the December 1918 edition of the quarterly publication of the Round Table group, pointed out the practical objections to the internationalization of the former German colonies and Turkish territories under the League of Nations. Instead, it advanced the proposal that "some democratic Power" be selected by the League to serve as a "guardian State" for each of the territories.[41]

For President Wilson, the type of administration which would replace German rule in its former colonies was one issue among many in late 1918. His comments on the topic suggest that he was weighing alternatives without being attached to any established position. At the same time, he seemed intent upon injecting into the colonial settlement some form of humanitarian international control which would prevent the

---

[39] George W. Egerton, *Great Britain and the Creation of the League of Nations: Strategy, Politics, and International Organization, 1914-1919* (Chapel Hill: University of North Carolina Press, 1978), p. 83.

[40] William Roger Louis, "The United States and the African Peace Settlement of 1919: The Pilgrimage of George Louis Beer," *Journal of African History* 4 (1963):415.

[41] "Windows of Freedom," *The Round Table: A Quarterly Review of the Politics of the British Empire* (December 1918):25-26.

looming Allied annexations from appearing to the public as simply an imperialist partition of the spoils of war.

Wilson provided a glimpse of his views in an interview with Sir William Wiseman on October 16, 1918. At the meeting, Wilson offered clarifications of the Fourteen Points. Among the other topics, Wiseman took note of the president's colonial attitude. Wilson criticized international commissions, opposed a return of the colonies to Germany and praised British colonial administration.

> He must warn the British, however, of the great jealousy of the other nations–including, he regretted to say, a large number of people in America. It would, he thought, create much bad feeling internationally if the German Colonies were handed over to us as a sovereign part of the British Empire. He wondered whether there was some way in which they could be administered in trust. "In trust," I asked, "for whom?" "Well, for the League of Nations, for instance," he said.[42]

At the end of October, Wilson approved the gloss on the Fourteen Points which had been prepared by Walter Lippmann and Frank Cobb. The two men, the secretary of the Inquiry and the editor of the *New York World* respectively, provided an interpretation of the Fourteen Points for Colonel House to use in negotiations with the Allied leaders in Paris.[43] Their com-

---

[42] Sir William Wiseman, "Notes on an interview with the President at the White House, Wednesday, October 16th, 1918," typescript copy in the House collection, Yale University Library, published by John L. Snell, "Document: Wilson on Germany and the Fourteen Points," *Journal of Modern History* 26 (December 1954):366-369. Wiseman, sent to the United States as British intelligence officer in 1915, had become a close friend of Colonel House, and together they formed the principal unofficial channel for Anglo-American discussions.

[43] Rudin, *Armistice 1918*, p. 267. House forwarded the gloss to Wilson

mentary on Point Five, which dealt with colonies, limited its application. It was to pertain only to the German colonies and other territories which might become objects of consideration due to the war. Consequently, it did not involve a "reopening of all colonial questions."[44]

The authors acknowledged the defense issues raised by the Allies and the economic concerns of the Germans. Finally, Lippmann and Cobb addressed the "interests of the populations," noting "that they should not be militarized, that exploitation should be conducted on the principle of the 'open door,'" and that the trustee should represent a capable authority willing to undertake development while protecting local customs.[45] These extrapolations of the American position formed the basis for House's armistice discussions with the Allies.

As the Wilson administration maneuvered toward a compromise with the Europeans, it also revealed an unwillingness to heed voices calling for a more active application of anti-imperialist policies. W.E.B. Du Bois put forward a program calling for the creation of a central African state to include the former German colonies, the Belgian Congo and in the future perhaps Portugal's possessions. Such a plan, he believed, would correspond with African desires. Du Bois's ideas, which

on October 29, and Wilson endorsed it as a "satisfactory interpretation of the principles" on the following day.

[44] Ibid., "Appendix E, Memorandum of Cobb and Lippmann on the Fourteen Points," p. 414.

[45] Ibid. Evidence that American views had not crystallized can be found in Klaus Schwabe, *Woodrow Wilson, Revolutionary Germany and Peacemaking, 1918-1919: Missionary Diplomacy and the Realities of Power* (Chapel Hill: University of North Carolina Press, 1985), pp. 82-83. Schwabe points out that in his discussion with Wiseman, Wilson categorically ruled out a return of the German colonies only under Germany's current form of government. Further, the Cobb-Lippmann gloss did not necessarily exclude Germany from the mandate system.

resemble those of the British Labour Party, were endorsed by the Board of Directors of the NAACP and submitted to the administration.[46] Although the proposal appears in accordance with the idealistic American rhetoric on self-determination, it proved too progressive to gain the administration's approval.

During the voyage of the *George Washington* to Europe, Wilson again set forth his ideas on how the former German colonies might be governed. On December 10, he held an hour-long conference with the chief specialists of the Inquiry. Beer's account of the meeting describes the "whole talk [as] frank, witty and full of charm" and portrays Wilson as "firm on broad general principles, but flexible as to their precise application."[47]

The future of the German colonies was the fourth major point on which the president focused. Wilson maintained his usual idealistic approach, assigning the colonial issue an importance transcending its own attributes. Beer summarized the president's new position:

> Common property will hold League together:
> e.g. German colonies. Evidently no idea of re-
> turning them. Their administration under man-
> date of League should be entrusted to some small
> state or several, e.g. Scandinavian, not to be a
> large one for fear that in latter event mandatory
> may develop into owner.[48]

---

[46] Clarence G. Contee, "Du Bois, the NAACP, and the Pan-African Congress of 1919," *Journal of Negro History* 57, 1 (January 1972):15-16. By the time the United States government responded, Du Bois already had left for Paris. There, despite American opposition, he organized the Pan-African Congress of 1919.

[47] George Louis Beer, Manuscript Diary, Library of Congress, Washington, D.C., p. 2.

[48] Ibid.

This final concept was both innovative and strikingly naive. That Wilson could have imagined, at this late date, that it would be possible to persuade the European powers to allow disinterested smaller states to administer the former German colonies reveals a lack of appreciation for the continuing strength of expansionist colonial attitudes in Europe and the British Empire.[49] Upon arriving in Europe, he would be quickly disabused of this notion.

Yet the president's assessment of the danger that would result from granting the mandates to the principal colonial states contained an element of validity. Wilson wanted the mandate system to be more than just a veiled form of annexation. Thus he arrived in Europe determined to forge a colonial settlement that would include a role for the League but with a certain flexibility as to how this might be accomplished.

At this point there began a period of critical interaction that eventually would produce a synthesis of Anglo-American mandate concepts. The mid-December advent of Wilson in Europe coincided with the publication of a tract, *The League of Nations: A Practical Suggestion*, by General Smuts. In his

---

[49] An example of the opposition to Wilson's proposal can be found in a letter from the French colonial minister to the foreign minister. The colonial minister reported that at the last meeting of the commission dealing with colonial questions, his department had learned of a conversation between President Wilson and the French ambassador in Washington, in which Wilson had advanced the idea of small states administering Germany's former colonies. According to the colonial minister, "it would be dangerous not to immediately dispel" such a suggestion which was not reconcilable with the limited capabilities of small powers. Further, he argued, it was necessary to assign the German colonies to those powers which had already shown their civilizing ability and which had a direct interest in the development of the territories because of their control of neighboring possessions. Le Ministre des colonies à Monsieur le Ministre des affaires étrangères, November 8, 1918, "Sort des colonies allemandes à l'issue de la guerre. Conversation entre M. Wilson et M. Jusserand," 1044 AP, ANSOM.

proposal, Smuts gave detailed consideration to the creation of a mandate system under the League.

Smuts suggested, "So far at any rate as the peoples and territories formerly belonging to Russia, Austria-Hungary and Turkey are concerned, the League of Nations should be considered as the reversionary in the most general sense." In contrast with the old policy of annexation by the victors, self-determination now was to be adopted as the guiding principle. Yet Smuts argued that because of differences in their levels of development, self-determination would not mean the same thing for all peoples. Some were capable of complete self-government, others autonomy, while in still other cases "autonomy in any real sense would be out of the question."[50]

Accordingly, the League would decide upon the future form of administration to be adopted in many of the areas. Smuts rejected direct international administration as impractical. Instead, he urged that the League make "use of the administrative organisation of individual States for the purpose." This could be accomplished "by nominating a particular State to act for and on behalf" of the League.[51]

Smuts's proposals, and especially the words he chose in presenting them, were to have lasting significance. Arriving in London in late December, Wilson was presented with a copy of *A Practical Suggestion*. "This document," writes George Curry, "more than any other of its kind, was to excite the imagination of the American President."[52]

Both Curry and Pitman Potter have pointed out that Wilson proceeded to incorporate, almost verbatim, sections of

---

[50] Jan C. Smuts, *The League of Nations: A Practical Suggestion* (London: Hodder and Stoughton, 1918), pp. 12-17.

[51] Ibid., p. 19.

[52] George Curry, "Woodrow Wilson, Jan Smuts, and the Versailles Settlement," *American Historical Review* 66 (July 1961):969.

Smuts's proposals into his Paris drafts of the League Covenant.[53] Nowhere was this more evident than in Wilson's supplementary clauses dealing with the mandate system.

There was, however, a major difference in Wilson's and Smuts's mandate systems. Smuts had excluded the German colonies. "The German colonies in the Pacific and Africa are inhabited by barbarians," he wrote, "who not only cannot possibly govern themselves, but to whom it would be impracticable to apply any ideas of political self-determination in the European sense."[54] Wilson, instead of accepting this position, included the German colonies in his mandate system. He thereby radically transformed Smuts's original program and set the stage for the first confrontation of the peace conference.[55]

Continental Strategies

As this evolving Anglo-American synthesis was producing a framework for the mandate system, French and Belgian war aims remained more tightly focused on Europe. Nevertheless, colonial enthusiasts pressed their governments not to abandon wartime acquisitions in Africa. Instead they regarded the conquests as their minimum desiderata, while continuing to contemplate major colonial exchanges favorable to their own empires. The climate of the time also forced them to offer arguments countering the Wilsonian challenge.

---

[53] Pitman B. Potter, "Origin of the System of Mandates under the League of Nations," *American Political Science Review* 16 (November 1922): 563-583. This article contains a detailed comparison of Smuts's and Wilson's views on the subject.

[54] Smuts, *A Practical Suggestion*, p. 15.

[55] Among those who emphasized the difference between their views was David Hunter Miller. "So Wilson did not take his ideas from Smuts, so far as the German Colonies were concerned; the Wilson idea was there the opposite of Smuts' idea." "The Origin of the Mandates System," *Foreign Affairs* (January 1928):281.

In France, Clemenceau remained firmly in charge of the government during the peace negotiations. Choosing to rely upon a few close advisers, particularly André Tardieu, he largely bypassed the chamber and the cabinet in developing policy. Unfettered, Clemenceau pursued two central, and frequently conflicting, objectives. Working to ensure the survival of Allied wartime solidarity, he also sought wherever possible to fortify France's own security.[56]

Colonial issues were of only collateral importance to Clemenceau, and he was not alone in assigning them a low priority.[57] Many on the French left opposed an imperialist peace settlement and supported Wilsonian ideals. A conversation between French socialist Albert Thomas and Beer on December 24 provides an accentuated illustration of these attitudes. According to Thomas, France primarily was concerned with domestic affairs and "not interested in colonial matters, except in two particulars, Morocco and a reversal of the Congo arrangement of 1911." France, he told Beer, was "*épuisée* [exhausted] and should avoid heavy administrative burdens in the colonial field or as mandatory."[58]

The various French colonialist societies remained divided over territorial priorities. Preferences for French acquisitions in the Levant competed with desires to unify French possessions in Africa. Even among those colonialists who focused their attention upon consolidating France's position in Africa, there remained the issue of whether to emphasize their interests in North Africa or those in the West and equatorial African confederations.[59]

---

[56] David Watson, *Georges Clemenceau: A Political Biography* (London: Eyre Methuen, 1974), pp. 338-339.

[57] David Heisser, "The Impact of the Great War on French Imperialism, 1914-1924" (Ph.D. thesis: University of North Carolina, Chapel Hill, 1972), p. 241.

[58] Beer, Manuscript Diary, pp. 6-7.

[59] This diffusion of demands is evident, for example, in the resolutions

There was greater consensus on the future of Germany's former colonies. Colonialists agreed that the territories should not be returned and that France should receive at least Togo and Cameroon. In November 1918, Camille Fidel's book, *La paix coloniale française*, was published. The most detailed statement of French colonial aspirations to appear during the armistice, it publicly advanced an imperialist rationale for the acquisition of the two colonies.

Military and moral reasons made the return of the colonies to Germany impossible, Fidel argued. Togo and Cameroon should be awarded to France as just compensation for the French military effort and Britain's colonial gains elsewhere. Those parts of French Equatorial Africa which had been incorporated into Cameroon in 1911 were "in truth an 'African Alsace-Lorraine,'" and restitution was taken for granted.[60]

The value of the two colonies for the French hinterland was also stressed. Fidel pointed out that if the reader glanced at a map and traced an imaginary line through the French posts of Fort-Lamy, Fort-Archambault, Fort-Crampel, Fort-de-Possel and Bangui, *"One would perceive that this line nearly takes the form of a semicircle of which the center is nothing other than the port of Douala*[emphasis in original]. Actually, as the crow flies, it is almost equidistant from each of the five

sent to the minister of foreign affairs by the *Comité de l'Afrique Française* and the *Comité du Maroc* on November 18, 1918. Insisting upon the "primary necessity of completing and consolidating French North Africa," the resolutions of the *Comité de l'Afrique Française* continued by stating the desire that colonial repartitions and exchanges in Africa assure France its just compensation. Yet these claims were stated in general terms, referring to geographically widespread territories. Le Président du *Comité du Maroc* and le Président du *Comité de l'Afrique Française* to M. le ministre des affaires étrangères, November 18, 1918, Afrique 1918-1919, Questions générales 1918 juin-décembre, 92, AMAE,F.

[60] Camille Fidel, *La paix coloniale française* (Paris: L. Tenin, 1918), p. 80.

French posts."[61] Depicting the port as the natural outlet for
French central Africa, Fidel described its acquisition as indispensable.

Within the French government, the most thorough effort to
formulate claims on the German colonies continued to be the
work at the Colonial Ministry of the *Commission d'étude des
questions coloniales posées par la guerre*. Still meeting under
the leadership of Gaston Doumergue in November 1918, the
commission sought to ensure that France would receive at least
Togo and Cameroon, with possible additional compensation
elsewhere.

A report prepared for the commission by Auguste Terrier examined the prospect that Germany might seek to recover its colonies at the peace conference. After describing
Germany's prewar colonial aspirations, Terrier turned to Germany's wartime colonial aims. He acknowledged that differences had existed between moderates in the German government and pan-German extremists who sought a German *Mittelafrika* and more. Yet he contended that if the Allies had not
won, the discord would have been replaced with exorbitant
colonial demands.[62]

The report's third part was designed to rebut German arguments for a return of their colonies. Terrier rejected German
claims that they had not undertaken military preparations in
their colonies and were not responsible for the spread of the
war to Africa. He likewise discounted the argument that the
performance of Germany's African troops deserved some compensation. Instead, he attributed von Lettow-Vorbeck's resistance to his ability to withdraw and the use of terror to ensure

---

[61] Ibid., p. 81.

[62] Auguste Terrier, "Les ambitions coloniales de l'Allemagne," Rapport
No. 17, *Commission d'étude des questions coloniales posées par la guerre*,
Paris, November 6-8, 1918, p. 63, 97 AP, ANSOM.

local support.[63] Finally, he dismissed any German rights based on prewar Anglo-German discussions.

To the contrary, Terrier stated three major reasons against a return of the colonies. First, through the construction of naval bases and the military training of African troops in any recovered colonies, Germany would create new threats for the Allies. Second, the Germans had proved incapable of understanding and administering colonial populations. Here Terrier not only called attention to the past atrocities of the Germans but also expressed concern for those Africans who had supported the Allies. The third argument was economic: "The Entente powers must reserve for themselves the production of African raw materials for the restoration of their economic prosperity endangered by four years of war."[64]

Terrier ended with a reminder of the policy pursued by German imperialists. The reciprocal justification it offered for the Allies was simply that of conquest, a concept as old as the history of war. "Let us return, in conclusion, to the German axiom of 1914: 'the fate of the the German colonies will be decided on the fields of battle in Europe.' It is therefore determined."[65]

The views of the commission were communicated to the colonial minister, Henri Simon, on November 13. Doumergue wrote to Simon that while the work of the commission had not yet been completed, he wished to inform the government of the conclusions reached on issues of current relevance.

He argued against internationalizing the former German colonies, including the indirect form of international administration which would place them under small powers. After re-

---

[63] Ibid., p. 69. The author observed, however: "It would without doubt have been otherwise if, from the beginning, the English had not set aside our offers of military collaboration in the conquest of East Africa."

[64] Ibid., p. 76.

[65] Ibid., pp. 76-77.

viewing the problems associated with these schemes, the commission had concluded that "the only rational decision consists in assigning the former German colonies to the Allied powers, which, having shown proof of their colonizing aptitude and their humane methods, would have possessions adjacent to the said colonies..."[66]

If this geographic rationale was logical, it was also self-serving. The commission believed France should be allowed to join Togo with its colony of Dahomey, and Cameroon with French Equatorial Africa. The acquisition of Togo would increase the size of the corridor to the interior formed by Dahomey and provide needed additional access to the sea. French control of Cameroon was necessary for the development of those French colonies which surrounded it. If another state received Cameroon, the progress of the French Congo would be dependent on it.

Elsewhere in the letter, Doumergue offered a creative economic reason for French acquisition of the former German colonies. Since France could expect to regain the provinces of Alsace and Lorraine, it was necessary to consider their commercial needs. Without sufficient overseas markets the inhabitants might make unpleasant comparisons with their prewar status.[67] Doumergue cautioned, however, that this was a justification that was likely to seem valid only in French eyes, and in negotiations with the Allies it was the German unfitness to colonize humanely which should be emphasized.

Simon's direction at the French Colonial Ministry followed the lines of his more experienced advisors on Africa. In mid-December, Simon sent a series of letters to French Foreign Minister Stephen Pichon expressing the Colonial Ministry's postwar desiderata. His letter of December 17 focused particularly on the future of the German colonies in Africa and echoed

---

[66] Doumergue to Simon, Paris, November 13, 1918, 97 AP, ANSOM.

[67] Ibid., p. 11.

many of Doumergue's arguments. Simon maintained that the alternative to annexation by Allied powers of proven colonial ability would be a paralyzed international administration.

Simon warned that there must be "absolute intransigence" in dispelling any consideration of returning the German colonies. Although mentioning that he had earlier given his reasons for this position, here he dealt at length with the unanimity of British opposition to any return. Not only did the British position conveniently correspond with the views of the French Colonial Ministry, it also provided the opportunity to combine French policy with an act of consideration due an ally.[68]

Contemporary Belgian colonial views reflected similar lines of development to those in France. With the war won, Colonial Ministry officials grasped at the apparent opportunity to make significant territorial gains. Colonial enthusiasts offered justifications for seeking the maximum additions to the Belgian Congo, while expounding upon the coveted areas' values. As in Paris, officials also sought to exculpate Belgium's performance as a colonial power with a civilizing mission.

In early November, a summary of the Belgian position was provided by the Foreign Ministry to the Belgian ambassador in Washington, D.C. The aim of this communication was to amend the views of the envoy, Baron Emile de Cartier de Marchienne, who apparently believed that Belgium intended to keep the territory it had conquered in Africa. The Foreign Ministry found this interpretation "too absolute," reminding the ambassador that all wartime occupation was considered provisional.[69]

---

[68] Simon to Pichon, "Sort à réserver aux colonies allemandes d'Afrique," Paris, December 17, 1918, 302, 1044 AP, ANSOM. "We have ourselves contracted an obligation toward the overseas British confederation, of which the sons have shed their blood on the soil of France, and we would be wrong to forget it in the moment of peace," exhorted Simon.

[69] Ministre des affaires étrangères à Mr. E. de Cartier de Marchienne,

In fact, the ambassador was informed that aside from frontier rectifications in the Lake Kivu region, "an extension of our colony in the east is not of essential importance to us. On the contrary, it is in the west that one finds the weak point of our colony."[70] Acquiring the left bank of the Congo was portrayed as Belgium's critical colonial interest.

Describing the Congo's port of Matadi as insufficient, the letter envisioned the construction of a new port in the territory Belgium hoped to acquire. Also, from a political viewpoint, Belgian possession of the left bank of the Congo was perceived as preventing any foreign power from gaining control of the area in the future and using it to dominate Belgium's colony.

To secure these Belgian aims on the Atlantic coast, the letter proposed a tripartite exchange. Belgium would cede conquered territory in East Africa to a third power, which would make concessions to Portugal, either in the region of Mozambique or elsewhere. In return, Belgium would receive the portion of northern Angola which it coveted. This scenario, with Britain acting as the intermediary, proved a surprisingly accurate sketch of Belgian colonial diplomacy at the Paris Peace Conference.

A far more detailed program for negotiating Belgium's African interests at the peace conference was developed by the Colonial Ministry. This extensive report was forwarded to Foreign Minister Hymans by the new colonial minister, Louis Franck, on December 24. In his cover letter, Franck outlined what he believed should be Belgium's principal colonial ob-

---

letter draft, "Nos desiderata coloniaux," Le Havre, November 12, 1918, Af 1/2 8659, AMAE,B. The Belgian policies outlined in the letter were described as for the ambassador's personal information, and he was instructed that any corresponding actions which he might undertake were to be of only an unofficial character.

[70] Ibid.

jectives in the peace negotiations, along with his reservations about some of the proposals in the detailed study.

As could be expected, Franck wrote that "In border rectifications, a priority should be placed on obtaining the left bank of the [Congo] river to the ocean." This he suggested could be accomplished according to the program in the accompanying position paper. In other areas the minister set forth his own ideas. He categorically rejected ceding any part of the Congo's territory. Belgium, he maintained, need not intervene in settling the general fate of the German colonies and should view with favor the East African expansion of its loyal ally, Great Britain.[71]

The last of these arguments may have been designed to counter the treatment of this issue in the detailed study. The report stated that the Belgian colonial ministry had no intention of directly opposing British policy in East Africa. Yet future strategic considerations gave cause for concern.

In the first place, "The attribution of German East Africa to the British Empire would make us neighbors of England from the Sudan to the western frontier of Rhodesia, and this especially would give to the British possessions in Africa a preponderance so great that the equilibrium would be upset." In addition, Britain was seen as already having the greatest influence in the area. This was because of the Union of South Africa, which it was believed could "become a cause of anxiety for the Congo." Concern that in certain circles there was emerging a "Monroe Doctrine" of South Africa heightened such apprehension.[72]

---

[71] Franck to Hymans, "Politique coloniale et revendications coloniales, 1916-1919," Brussels, December 24, 1918, Papiers Orts, 433, AGR. A copy of the letter, dated December 23, also is found in the Foreign Ministry Archives: Af 1/2 8685, AMAE,B.

[72] "Programme des revendications de la Belgique dans le domaine colonial," Première partie, Principes généraux, p. 40, Papiers Orts, 433, AGR.

Britain's great interest in retaining "our common conquest" was seen as resulting from three motives. First, it would allow the construction "through exclusively British territory of the Cape-to-Cairo railway, symbol of British supremacy in Africa." It also would assure Britain of "absolute control in the Indian Ocean." Finally, the acquisition of German East Africa would unify Britain's vast African possessions and establish British supremacy in East Africa, and "one could say throughout all of Africa."[73]

Belgium, the report suggested, should strive to satisfy these British objectives in a manner which would protect its own interests. The connecting link between Britain's African possessions could be provided by ceding to Britain territory between the northern end of Lake Tanganyika and Uganda. Steamship service on the lake might then connect British railways at both ends. The additional cession to Britain of Dar es Salaam would guarantee British control of the Indian Ocean.

What remained of German East Africa could be used to serve Belgium's purposes. As compensation for Portuguese concessions to Belgium on Africa's west coast, Portugal was to receive territory lying north of Mozambique. The rest of Germany's former colony then could be assigned to a power which would not seek hegemony in the area, and an equilibrium in the region would be established. With this purpose in mind, two powers were proposed: the Netherlands and Italy.

The choice of the Netherlands would contain potential benefits for Belgium in Europe. "Could not German East Africa be ceded to them in exchange for the left bank of the Scheldt, which they would hand over to us?"[74] The captured German

---

[73] Ibid., p. 42.

[74] Ibid., p. 46. For a discussion of Belgian territorial aims in Europe, see Sally Marks, *Innocent Abroad: Belgium at the Paris Peace Conference of 1919* (Chapel Hill: University of North Carolina Press, 1981), pp. 137-169.

colony thus might be transformed into a bargaining chip for delivering to Belgium the coveted Dutch provinces of Flemish Zeeland.

Despite such an auspicious prospect, a Dutch presence in Africa also could have an unknown effect on Belgium's position in the Congo. Belgian objections would be raised because of the "affinities which exist between the Dutch and the Boers of the Transvaal. But, this affinity can also exercise a pacifying influence."[75] Nevertheless, Italy seemed to be the preferable choice, for it offered Britain and France the opportunity to fulfill their imperialist obligations resulting from the Treaty of London in 1915.

The examination of the issue concluded with a discussion of the compatibility of proposals in the report with the ideas of President Wilson, and a warning that Belgium must act with great delicacy, particularly to avoid offending Great Britain. Visible throughout this analysis of conceivable East African peace settlements is a strong element of continuity with earlier Belgian colonial policy. The apprehension of Belgian officials over future South African actions, and their desire to establish a new political equilibrium in Africa, represent fresh manifestations of the small state's long-standing concern over the intentions of other colonial powers toward its giant African colony.

The second part of the report emphatically restated the preponderant Belgian colonial objective. "The essential, major frontier rectification that we must pursue is that of the mouth of the Congo. This objective must take precedence over all the others, and it is to attain it that our principal efforts must lead."[76] A detailed assessment of the existing border's com-

---

[75] "Programme des revendications," p. 46, Papiers Orts, AGR.

[76] "Seconde partie. Programme des revendications concrètes de la Belgique en matière coloniale," p. 71, ibid.

mercial and military disadvantages followed, and this led to a series of proposals for specific boundary changes. All of these would have pushed Angola's northern border to the south, with the optimum solution ceding the entire northern district of the Portuguese Congo to Belgium. The division of the Cabinda enclave between France and Belgium also was envisioned.

In East Africa, it was hoped that commercial advantages along the Central Railway from Kigoma to Dar es Salaam could be obtained. Retaining Ruanda, however, was secondary to the foregoing primary objective of Belgian colonial policy. Yet the Colonial Ministry affirmed that "If the powers refused it these satisfactions, Belgium would have to conserve its conquest. This is the common law."[77]

Elsewhere, the report pointedly rejected the concept of internationalizing colonies in tropical Africa and sought freedom from earlier international restrictions on the Belgian Congo. A speech by former Colonial Minister Jules Renkin defending Belgian colonization was quoted at length as justification.[78] Given the past criticism of their policies, the Belgians naturally were sensitive about this issue.

The related question of African interests in the captured German colonies was addressed in a letter from the Colonial Ministry to the foreign minister. In common with their counterparts in other Allied countries, Belgian officials felt compelled to produce evidence that, indeed, Africans desired Belgian rule.

Accordingly, an affirmation of this was generated in Ruanda. Juhi IV Mussinga, the sultan of Ruanda, had been assisted by the Germans in consolidating his authority before the war. Now he reportedly solicited Belgian administration:

> I have learned by a soldier from Nyansa that July 1st is a Congo holiday and that this holiday is for

---

[77] Ibid., p. 79.
[78] Ibid., pp. 55-56.

remembering the day when Boula-Matari considered the Congo as a part of Belgium.

I also desire to tell you that I would greatly rejoice that Boula-Matari would consider me the same. It has built schools in all places and many already know how to read and write. At the same time, I recall that the Germans did not pay attention to my affairs. They left me as a wild animal.[79]

To the extent that this was an accurate representation of Mussinga's views, it is perhaps best explained by another observation of Charles Dundas: "Africans are not so simple as to tell the victor that they prefer to be ruled by the vanquished."[80] In terms of Belgian policy, the letter represents the perceived necessity of proceeding along the same path as Britain and France, screening imperialist expansion in altruistic terms.

---

[79] Translation by Captain P. Reindl from Kiswahili on July 15, 1918; the document, along with a cover letter, was sent from the general secretary of the Colonial Ministry to the foreign minister on December 31, 1918. Af 1/2 8688, AMAE,B.

[80] Dundas, *African Crossroads*, p. 106.

5

The Paris Peace Conference

Confrontation and Conciliation: January 1919

The Paris Peace Conference opened on January 12, 1919, meeting at the Quai d'Orsay. Despite the host of pressing questions facing the assembled leaders, the basic structure of the mandate system had been created by the end of the month.

Lloyd George was the driving force behind this rapid settlement. Motivated by the British desire to indemnify the southern Dominions for their participation in the war, the prime minister sought to arrange an early disposition of the German colonies. In this policy, his primary concern was to see that the Union of South Africa, Australia and New Zealand received the possessions they respectively coveted: German Southwest Africa, New Guinea and Samoa.

Maneuvering the issue into the discussions of the Council of Ten on January 24, Lloyd George quickly won agreement from the other major powers that none of the colonies would be returned to Germany.[1] The British prime minister then presented his views on the options for their future administration.

---

[1] U.S. Department of State, *Papers Relating to the Foreign Relations of the United States, The Paris Peace Conference, 1919 (FRUS)*, 13 vols. (Washington, D.C.: Government Printing Office, 1942-47), 3:718-719. Public announcement of the decision not to restore Germany's colonies was withheld at this time.

He dismissed international control in a cursory fashion. The mandate concept, however, he was willing to accept on behalf of Britain. In Lloyd George's opinion, it "did not differ materially from the method in which the British Empire dealt with its Colonies."[2]

In the territories occupied by the southern Dominions, Lloyd George reasoned that outright annexation would be more appropriate. The Dominions then individually presented their claims. Primarily basing their arguments for annexation on strategic concerns and physical proximity, they also recalled the sacrifices their states had made during the war.

Speaking for the Union of South Africa, General Smuts sought to persuade his listeners of the differences between German Southwest Africa and the other German colonies on the continent. "The Cameroons, Togo-land and East Africa were all tropical and valuable possessions; South-West Africa was a desert country without any product of great value and only suitable for pastoralists." Given these circumstances, he argued that the Union was the logical choice for developing its neigh-

---

[2] Ibid. Philip Kerr, Lloyd George's adviser, provided a glimpse of this British view in a confidential letter to Lord Milner, now colonial secretary:

> ... the only way in which you can apply the mandatory principle at all was on the lines which have been worked out by practical experience in the British Empire, namely that you select your mandatory power, impose certain conditions upon it in regard to arms traffic, liquor traffic, slave trade, and the open door, and then make it fully responsible for the good government of its trustee territories, subject to the liability of being criticised at the meetings of the League of Nations by the other members of the League in the event of its failure to live up to its obligations.

Kerr to Milner, January 31, 1919, MSS English History, c. 700, BLO. The letter is in a collection of additional Milner papers given to the Bodleian Library in 1973.

bor, and while mandates might be suitable for other parts of Africa "there was not, in this instance, a strong case."[3]

The British Empire thus divided its claims to the German colonies. The Dominions pushed for direct annexation of the territories they hoped to acquire, while Britain agreed to act as mandatory in East Africa. Even there British decision makers envisioned a closely circumscribed League role, one that would complement rather than interfere with British colonial administration.

In Cameroon and Togo, the French sought even less international oversight and adopted an openly annexationist approach. Addressing the Council of Ten on January 28, French Colonial Minister Simon stated his nation's pretensions to the two colonies. He argued that France was entitled to "them for the same reasons that had been used by the Dominions." Simon recalled French wartime sacrifices as well as France's historical claims to the territories.

The Australian prime minister's arguments of "economic and geographical contiguity" also served as justifications for French annexation. "The large sea coast of the Cameroons, and the port of Duala were required for the development of French Equatorial Africa," declared the French colonial minister.[4]

After supporting the Dominions' objections to internationalization and trusteeship, Simon defended French colonial policies. He promised that France would protect the rights of the inhabitants in Togo and Cameroon and that free trade practices would be adopted in the two colonies. Thus, the second half of his speech attempted to present French claims in the most politically palatable fashion.

---

[3] *FRUS*, 3:722-723. Smuts's appraisal of Southwest Africa was both misleading and inaccurate; diamonds already were being mined productively in the territory. See Ruth First, *South West Africa* (Baltimore: Penguin Books, 1963), pp. 87-88.

[4] *FRUS*, 3:760.

President Wilson, who up to this point had defended his concept of mandates against the Dominions' position, now clearly rejected what he perceived to be blatant colonial expansionism. He observed that "the discussion so far had been, in essence, a negation in detail – one case at a time – of the whole principle of mandatories. The discussion had been brought to a point where it looked as if their roads diverged."[5]

British Foreign Secretary Balfour and Lloyd George intervened, seeking to appease the American president while still achieving their aims. Lloyd George argued that Britain had expressed willingness to administer German East Africa under the League and that Simon "had detailed as acceptable to France the whole list of conditions proposed for a mandatory, except the name." But Wilson would have none of this explanation. He was pleased by British willingness to accept the principle of trusteeship in East Africa, but this was "the only exception to the rejection of the idea.... The world would say that the Great Powers first portioned out the helpless parts of the world, and then formed a League of Nations."[6]

Clemenceau then responded to Wilson's position in a conciliatory manner. This was completely in keeping with his own attitude of assigning colonial objectives a subordinate position within French foreign policy. Just as Simon's presentation had represented the French colonial ministry's annexationist ambitions in Africa, Clemenceau's European focus allowed him to abandon them.[7] He observed that Lloyd George had interpreted Simon's speech better than Wilson and that he agreed with Wilson's sentiments.

---

[5] Ibid., p. 763.

[6] Ibid., pp. 767-768.

[7] Pierre Miquel has pointed out that these attitudes also were reflected in the French press. Although the colonialist journals opposed the mandate system, the press in general did not place great emphasis on the division of the German colonies. *La Paix de Versailles et l'opinion publique française*, (Paris: Flammarion, 1972), pp. 182-183.

Clemenceau expressed a willingness to make concessions "if reasonable proposals were put forward." In a diplomatic fashion, clearly designed to placate both of his allies, the French premier continued:

> He did not regret the discussions which had taken place on the subject, since these discussions had impressed him with the justness of the claims of the Dominions. However, since Mr. Lloyd George was prepared to accept the mandate of the League of Nations he would not dissent from the general agreement, merely for the sake of the Cameroons and Togoland.[8]

Shortly thereafter the meeting was adjourned until the following day, without a decision having been taken on the mandate concept. Yet it is evident that during the meeting of January 28 France had joined Britain, accepting in principle the application of the mandatory idea to the former German colonies of tropical Africa.

The central arena for the formulation of the League mandate system now shifted to the internal meetings of the British Empire delegation. In the next two days, a carefully crafted compromise plan was devised which formed the basis of the future three-tier mandate system, later designated A, B and C mandates.

Dividing the conquered territories on the basis of their locations, and what imperial statesmen perceived to be the comparative inability of the indigenous populations to direct their own governments, the territories were to be assigned to one of the three types. The plan allowed the mandatory states to arrogate increasingly greater control to themselves as they

---

[8] *FRUS*, 3:768-769. Following Clemenceau's statement, Lloyd George asked him if he accepted "trusteeship." Clemenceau answered that "although he did not approve of it, he would be guided by the judgment of his colleagues." p. 770.

moved from the A to C mandates. Eventually the former Arab provinces of the Ottoman Empire were to form the A mandates and Germany's tropical African colonies the B mandates. The C mandates, conceived as little more than a veiled form of annexation, were to be composed of the territories coveted by the southern Dominions.

A certain obscurity still surrounds the explicit authorship of the draft mandate proposals. In his comprehensive and confidential letter to Lord Milner on the topic, Kerr wrote:

> There were several meetings of the Imperial delegation and finally the Prime Minister, after something of a row with Hughes, got them to agree to resolutions whereby the mandatory idea was accepted as a general principle for ex Turkish and Central African German possessions, but that certain of the South Pacific islands and the South West African territories were placed in a category which made them practically integral parts of the mandatory power.[9]

Hessel Duncan Hall, an Australian historian of the topic, reports that the British delegation created a committee on mandates composed of the prime ministers of the southern Dominions. "Next morning 29 January Lloyd George had in his hands a complete mandates draft."[10] Smuts gained Colonel

---

[9] Kerr to Milner, January 31, 1919, MSS English History c. 700, BLO. The purpose of the letter is described in its opening sentence: "The Prime Minister has asked me to write and let you know what really happened about the disposition of the ex-German Colonies at the Peace Conference..."

[10] Hessel Duncan Hall, "The British Commonwealth and the Founding of the League Mandate System," *Studies in International History*, ed. K. Bourne and D.C. Watt (Hamden, Conn.: Archon Books, 1967), p. 357. Hall writes that while authorship traditionally has been assigned to Smuts and Philip Kerr, the formula for at least the C mandates was the work of an Australian, J.G. Latham. Consequently, Hall criticizes those authors

House's acceptance of the draft, and it was then approved by the British Empire delegation.[11]

On the following morning, Lloyd George formally presented the draft to the Council of Ten. He warned that it represented a compromise, an observation upon which Hughes elaborated by repeating the Australian preference for direct control. Wilson replied by objecting bitterly about press leaks but noting that he considered the draft "a very gratifying paper. It made a long stride towards the composition of their differences, bringing them to within an easy stage of final agreement."[12]

When the dust had settled, this proved to be in large part true. On January 30, however, the ensuing discussion was marked by a sharp clash between Wilson and Hughes. The American president insisted that mandate decisions taken at this point be provisional. This position infuriated leaders of the Dominions, who believed that in return for yielding on annexation, they should immediately be granted mandates for the territories they desired.

The focus of this debate was the C mandates. In the end, Lloyd George proposed provisional acceptance, to which the

---

who have described the draft as Smuts's plan. A role in developing the compromise also has been attributed to Sir Maurice Hankey, the secretary of the British delegation, by his biographer. Stephen Roskill, *Hankey: Man of Secrets*, 3 vols., (London: Collins, 1970-74) 2:54. Hankey himself wrote that at this point during the conference he was eating every meal with Lloyd George in order to solve the problems over the German colonies. He later stated only that agreement on the draft was reached "after several exhaustive discussions." Hankey, *The Supreme Control at the Paris Peace Conference 1919: A Commentary* (London: Allen Unwin, 1963), pp. 60-61.

[11] Arthur Walworth, *Wilson and His Peacemakers: American Diplomacy at the Paris Peace Conference, 1919* (New York: W.W. Norton and Co., 1986), pp. 76-77.

[12] *FRUS*, 3:787.

other powers agreed.[13] Later, this provisional settlement was adopted nearly verbatim into the relevant articles of the League Covenant (Article XVII, later Article XXII).

Paragraph seven of the British draft dealt specifically with Germany's former tropical African colonies. It read:

> They [the Allied and Associated Powers] further consider that other peoples, especially those of Central Africa, are at such a stage that the mandatory must be responsible for the the administration of the territory subject to conditions which will guarantee the prohibition of abuses such as the slave trade, the arms traffic and the liquor traffic, and the prevention of the military training of the natives for other than police purposes, and the establishment of fortifications or military and naval bases, and will also secure equal opportunities for the trade and commerce of other members of the League of Nations.[14]

The proposed wording of this clause led to further discord at the highest political level over the conditions of the mandates to be applied in Cameroon and Togo. During the after-

---

[13] Paul Birdsall has pointed out that this was actually Wilson's position earlier in the day. The author makes a strong case that despite the concessions Wilson was forced to make, the creation of the mandate system was a major accomplishment for the president. *Versailles Twenty Years After* (New York: Reynal and Hitchcock, 1941), pp. 73-75. Arthur S. Link, too, believes the mandate system was a significant victory for Wilson. *Wilson the Diplomatist* (Baltimore: Johns Hopkins Press, 1957; reprint ed., New York: New Viewpoints, 1974), p. 113. It should be added that Wilson's advocacy of the mandate system also was opposed by his secretary of state, Robert Lansing. For Lansing's position see his book, *The Peace Negotiations* (Boston: Houghton Mifflin, 1921), Chapter XIII "The System of Mandates," pp. 149-161.

[14] *FRUS*, 3:796.

noon meeting of the council on January 30, Canadian Prime Minister Robert Borden suggested changing the paragraph to make more precise the prohibition against using this class of mandates for military purposes. President Wilson welcomed the semantic change.

The French, however, quickly sought to protect their right to raise troops in the mandates. Foreign Minister Pichon and Clemenceau both spoke of the need for France to be able to recruit volunteers in all the territories under its colonial control. Lloyd George, again playing the role of conciliator, sought a mutually acceptable explanation. The aim of the clause, he argued, was to prevent colonial powers from "raising great native armies against each other.... There was nothing in this document which prevented France doing what she did before. The defence of the territory was provided for."[15] Clemenceau accepted this position, with the rejoinder that "if he could raise troops, that was all he wanted." A brief discussion of the issue ensued, apparently resolving the question along the lines suggested by Lloyd George.[16] In fact, the wording remained vague enough to provide illusory agreement while allowing different interpretations. Later, experts and diplomats would quarrel over the actual meaning with regard to the recruiting and use of troops from the French mandates.

If the French displayed their desire to treat the mandates as colonies by using them equally as reservoirs of military manpower, Lloyd George indicated his reluctance to make concessions in East Africa when the Belgians were allowed to address the council. Their hearing late on January 30 came at the insistence of the French and despite the disapproval of both Lloyd George and Wilson.

Represented by Pierre Orts, the Belgians claimed that their involvement in central Africa and participation in the war effort

---

[15] Ibid., p. 804.
[16] Ibid., pp. 804-805.

there entitled them to a voice in the disposition of the German colonies. Orts detailed the military campaigns of the Belgian Congo and described the insecurity Belgium felt over German colonial intentions.

Consequently, Belgium hoped Germany would cease to be its colonial neighbor. The Belgians, Orts continued:

> had no desire for conquest, but they thought it would be only fair in view of all the losses they had sustained, and it would complete the Congo Colony in many respects, if they could be allowed to retain permanently under their administration the territories in East Africa which they now provisionally occupied.[17]

When Orts had finished, Lloyd George intervened. He argued that since mandates were not being assigned at this point, the Belgians were asking for something that was not under discussion. Furthermore, observed Lloyd George, "Belgium asked for the most fertile portion of East Africa whereas they had not made good use of what they had on the Western side."[18]

This critical remark soon found its way to the Belgians, where it provoked an indignant reaction. In a conversation on February 8, Emmanuel de Peretti, chief of the African department at the French Foreign Ministry, repeated the comment to Octave Louwers. Louwers, who had been attached to the Belgian delegation for work on colonial issues, replied angrily: "We have paid for these territories with our efforts, and the lives of many of our soldiers. Even more, without our cooperation it is probable that the English would not have succeeded in conquering East Africa."

"I know," de Peretti responded sympathetically. "I am telling you the opinion of Mr. Lloyd George. As for us, we

---

[17] Ibid., p. 812.
[18] Ibid., pp. 812-813.

were very pleased with the statement of M. Orts."[19]

In the broader picture, the general attitude of British and French statesmen toward the mandate system can be discerned. Both states proved willing to accept it. This was particularly true in tropical Africa, which neither power viewed as a geographical priority. The continuing colonial scramble for territory in East and West Africa had been only submerged, however, under discussion of the mandates.[20] The division of Germany's former tropical African possessions now proceeded, as the British, French and Belgians vigorously strove to attain their colonial objectives.

The Council of Four

The decisions reached by the Council of Ten in late January represented only a general theoretical framework for the mandate system. In this form the mandates were included in the provisional draft of the League Covenant presented by

---

[19] Note by Louwers describing his conversation with de Peretti, February 8, 1919, Af 1/2, AMAE,B. Earlier in the meeting, Louwers provided an equally revealing insight into the Belgian attitude toward East Africa. "Nevertheless, we have conquered a territory (I know that the word sounds bad in the terminology of the Conference, but between us we can use it) we occupy this territory, we have laid claim to the free and eventual administration of it, and we do not intend to abandon it."

[20] My research indicates that colonial competition in tropical Africa remained a characteristic of Allied policy. This contradicts the earlier assertion of Ernst B. Haas: "It is true that while there was no interallied rivalry of any kind with respect to the division of spoils in Africa and the Pacific, there did exist a definite rivalry between France and the United Kingdom in the Middle East." "The Reconciliation of Conflicting Colonial Policy Aims: Acceptance of the League of Nations Mandate System," *International Organization* 6 (November 1952):531.

President Wilson to the third plenary session of the peace conference on February 14 and approved in the final draft of the covenant at the fifth plenary session on April 28.

Forging the colonial peace settlement for tropical Africa, however, involved a great deal more negotiation. It required three commissions and two sets of bilateral negotiations (British-French and British-Belgian). Among these elements, the bilateral negotiations proved to be the primary channels for actually dividing the former German colonies. Meeting during the spring of 1919, Colonial Ministry officials and experts drew the new boundaries that repartitioned tropical Africa.

Yet in the midst of these negotiations, the occasion arose when the mandate question again demanded the focused attention of the Allied leaders. By examining first the discussions and decisions of the Council of Four in early May, the course of each of the negotiations can be traced with continuity.

Formed as a streamlined executive for the peace conference, composed of Wilson, Lloyd George, Clemenceau and Italian Premier Vittorio Orlando, the Council of Four was at the beginning of May actually a Council of Three. Having quarreled with the other members, particularly Wilson, over the Adriatic settlement, Orlando had returned temporarily to Italy. In this setting the colonial conflicts of late January resurfaced.

The Peace Conference Commission on German Colonies had at its meeting of April 24, 1919, adopted the clause: "Germany renounces, in favor of the Five Allied and Associated Powers, all its rights and titles to its overseas possessions."[21] News of this decision heightened Belgian fears of being excluded from the impending East African settlement. The wording implied that sovereignty would be transferred to the five great powers – Britain, France, Italy, the United States and

---

[21] Commission on German Claims, Peace Conference, Procès Verbal, Session of April 24, 1919, File Number 181.22601/1, National Archives, Washington, D.C. (NA).

Japan. Alarmed, Belgian Premier Hymans expressed these concerns in a letter to Clemenceau, who raised the issue at the council meeting of May 2.

Lloyd George quickly vetoed the simple solution of including other powers in the clause. Belgium, he observed, was putting forth "a most impudent claim. At a time when the British Empire had millions of soldiers fighting for Belgium, a few black troops had been sent into German East Africa."[22]

Wilson and Lloyd George then argued that since mandates were not being allocated by the clause, it was an inappropriate context for registering the Belgian claim. Following Wilson's suggestion, Clemenceau agreed to inform the Belgians that their interests would be considered by the Council of the League of Nations, where they would be represented.

With Belgian demands seemingly quieted, Lloyd George performed a swift pirouette. On May 5, he pushed for a rapid mandate settlement. Focusing on the German colonies, the British prime minister explained that he was "most anxious to be able to announce the mandates to the Press at the time when the Peace Treaty was issued." Although Wilson responded with apprehension that "he was very anxious to avoid the appearance of a division of the spoils being simultaneous with the Peace," Clemenceau adopted an accommodating atti-

---

[22] *FRUS*, 5:419-420. A Belgian reaction was recorded by George Louis Beer, whom the Belgians consulted over the issue on the following day. "Van den Ven [a professor at the University of Louvain and a special delegate for the Belgian Ministry of Finance] was bitter about English attitude towards Belgium on reparations saying they were insatiable, 'cochons,' etc., and that he would not trust them to treat Belgium fairly in Africa. What a dreadful mass of hatred this war and the negotiations for peace have engendered." Beer, while willing to accept conciliatory wording in the clause, also noted that "personally I am opposed to giving any (more) of German East Africa to Belgium. They have more of Africa than they can administer properly." May 3, 1919, Beer, Manuscript Diary.

tude.[23] Consequently, a detailed discussion of the former German colonies took place on the following day.

According to Lloyd George, the only difficulties arose over the division and status of Cameroon and Togo. British Colonial Secretary Milner having returned home, Simon was summoned to explain what arrangements had been made.[24] The French colonial minister outlined Anglo-French negotiations on the subject. He believed agreement over the division of Cameroon had been reached, but the discussions with regard to the partition of Togo remained inconclusive.

Lloyd George then proposed that France should receive the mandate for Cameroon, with the understanding that there would be a rectification of the border with Nigeria. In the case of Togo, he opposed mandates, arguing that "the country was cut into small bits, and it would be found that half of a tribe was under a mandate, and the other was not." Wilson, consistent with his adherence to the universality of the mandate principle, resisted this departure.[25] Discussion then concluded with agreement that Simon prepare, by the following day, a formula along the lines suggested by Lloyd George.

---

[23] *FRUS*, 5:472-473.

[24] Milner had served as secretary of state for war before the formation of Lloyd George's new ministry in January 1919. He was not selected as one of the British Empire's five chief delegates to the peace conference but was to play a large role in the colonial settlement. See A.M. Gollin, *Proconsul in Politics: A Study of Lord Milner in Opposition and in Power* (London: A. Blond, 1964), pp. 584-586.

[25] *FRUS*, 5:493. Even more than the official minutes kept by Sir Maurice Hankey, which are the source for *FRUS*, the French translator's account portrays Wilson as insisting that the mandatory principle be applied to all of the German territories, including the section of Cameroon which Britain received. Paul Mantoux, *Les délibérations du conseil des quatre*, 2 vols. (Paris: Éditions du centre national de la recherche scientifique, 1955), 1:502.

With an apparent settlement close on May 7, clashing imperialist ambitions still required conciliation. Simon sought to recover the Cameroon territory ceded by France in 1911 in full sovereignty. At the same time, he objected to Britain receiving the area along the Nigerian border without it being held under a mandate. Lloyd George and Balfour endeavored to counter these arguments, but in the end the British prime minister proposed compromise language.[26]

The Italians having returned to the Council, a new question now arose. Orlando complained that Italy was being excluded from the mandates in Africa, while under Article Thirteen of the Treaty of London it was entitled to colonial compensation if Britain and France increased their African empires at the expense of Germany. Lloyd George and Clemenceau readily recognized the general validity of the Italian claim and agreed to discussions.[27]

With these hurdles overcome, the mandates were assigned.[28] In tropical Africa, Britain and France were to make a joint recommendation to the League on the future of Togo and Cameroon, while Britain received the mandate for German East Africa.

This provoked a further dispute. On the following day, Hymans read in the papers that Belgium had not been included as an East African mandatory, and he immediately protested.[29] On May 9, he was received in impromptu fashion by the Council of Four. Clemenceau and Wilson admitted they were unin-

---

[26] FRUS, 5:506-07 and Mantoux, 1:513-514.

[27] This led to the creation of the second peace conference commission to deal with Germany's former African possessions, the Commission on Colonies. For a detailed analysis of the Italian claims see Robert L. Hess, "Italy and Africa," pp. 119-126.

[28] FRUS, 5:508.

[29] Marks, Innocent Abroad, p. 319.

formed on the particulars of the situation and referred him to Lloyd George.

Lloyd George, too, claimed to be ignorant of the Belgian campaign in East Africa. He agreed, however, to recall Milner to Paris so the issue might be settled.[30] In view of the British prime minister's earlier positions, it seems logical to assume that Lloyd George's ignorance was at least in part feigned and that his willingness to continue discussions was designed to avoid quarreling with a small power which was viewed sympathetically by much of the Allied public.

West Africa

As Simon mentioned to the Council of Four, Anglo-French talks over the partition of Togo and Cameroon already had begun. Starting from the provisional divisions made during the war, French negotiators sought to increase their share, particularly with the aim of securing the routes to their colonies in the interior of Africa. The British proved willing to acquiesce on this primary French objective but bargained for territorial compensation.

Simon and Milner along with their assistants met on March 6, and both sides stated their colonial desiderata. According to Simon, the French were prepared to be "very accommodating in the Cameroons, but could not adopt quite the same policy in Togoland." By this he meant that in Cameroon the French were generally willing to accept the provisional border, but they hoped to extend the railway running northward and desired some territorial concessions along the route. Although this conflicted with British ambitions at the town of Dschang, Simon agreed to make no difficulty over the inclusion of all of German Bornu in the British sphere.

---

[30] Louis, *Ruanda-Urundi 1884-1919*, pp. 238-239.

Regarding Togo, on the other hand, Simon stated that: "France wanted the whole of it. He supported the demand mainly on the ground that Dahomey had a very small seaboard (some 70 miles) and urgently required more – Dahomey formed a narrow corridor and was in danger of being stifled."[31]

Milner found the French claim unreasonable, particularly in light of what he regarded as Britain's "extreme accommodation" in Cameroon. Unmoved, Simon pointed to Britain's additional acquisitions in Africa and elsewhere. He protested further when presented with the maximum British aspirations in Togo.

Following this joint effort to demonstrate the seriousness of their national claims and to rebut the other's contentions, Simon and Milner moved gingerly toward compromise positions. They concluded the session by outlining the concessions they might be willing to make. Simon offered to agree to British requests in the north of Togo in return for Lomé and the railways. Milner responded that:

> it was quite beyond his competence to give away
> Lome and the railways, but that if, as part of
> a general settlement this were ever done, then
> France having the lion's share of both these Colo-
> nies would certainly be expected to settle all mi-
> nor points, such as the rectification of tribal bound-
> aries in our favour.[32]

After the Council of Four had made its mandate decisions, talks resumed. On May 20, Milner met with Simon at the French Colonial Ministry and the French produced a new map containing their boundary proposals. Negotiations now passed into the hands of colonial experts who sought to achieve their concrete objectives through the process of careful and definitive

---

[31] "Cameroons and Togoland," notes on the meeting by C. Strachey, May 7, 1919, Milner Papers, 389:61b-d, BLO.

[32] Ibid.

frontier delimitation. The French relied on individuals long active in West African affairs: Albert Duchêne, chief of the African department at the Colonial Ministry, and the former governor general of French Equatorial Africa, M.H. Merlin.

Milner was assisted by Sir Herbert Read of the Colonial Office and an adviser of particular expertise in West Africa, Charles Strachey. A career Colonial Office official, Strachey had traveled in Nigeria during 1914. Among other duties, Strachey had served as a delegate to the Anglo-German boundary conferences (Yola-Chad, March 1906 and Yola to the sea, October 1909) which had dealt with the border between Nigeria and Cameroon. Consequently, upon receiving the French map of May 20, he was well prepared to begin a careful analysis of it and to develop detailed counterproposals.

The French map of Togo was a small inset on the larger Cameroon map. Strachey transferred the border which the French proposed to a larger-scale map of Togo and included other factors he believed pertinent to making a British decision. A line supplied by the governor of the Gold Coast, Sir Hugh Clifford, was drawn representing Britain's minimum desiderata. Based on accommodating the French demand for Lomé and the railways, its aim was to "improve the existing Anglo-German boundary and reunite to their tribal chiefs on the British side of the boundary as many as possible of the lands and villages which had been cut off and placed under German rule."[33]

In the south of Togo the British and French lines coincided, while Britain gained from the French proposal in the center of the country, and France benefited in the north. The deciding factor in the north proved to be the French desire to extend the German railway into French West Africa. The French had

---

[33] "French Proposal for Partition of Togoland," C. Strachey, May 23, 1919, FO 608/216/70142, PRO.

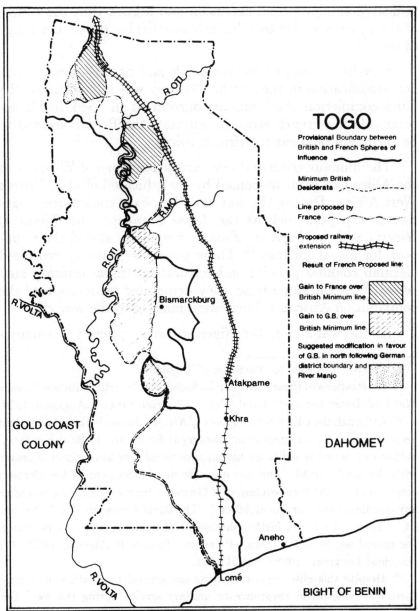

TOGO

Provisional Boundary between British and French Spheres of Influence

Minimum British Desiderata

Line proposed by France

Proposed railway extension

Result of French Proposed line:

Gain to France over British Minimum line

Gain to G.B. over British Minimum line

Suggested modification in favour of G.B. in north following German district boundary and River Manjo

R. OTI

R.MO

R. OTI

R. VOLTA

Bismarckburg

GOLD COAST COLONY

DAHOMEY

Atakpame

Khra

Aneho

R. VOLTA

Lomé

BIGHT OF BENIN

Partition of Togo 1919. Source: MPK 272(4) (FO 608/216), PRO.

indicated this proposed extension and argued that the course of the route was due to "the only practicable pass" in a range of hills.[34]

Strachey thought this reasonable and proposed only a minor modification in the north. The way was now open for the quick completion of a boundary agreement on Togo, but in accommodating French strategic interests the British seemed to be turning a deaf ear to African voices.

The humanitarian and democratic language of Wilson and the Allies had been welcomed by the educated elite in British West Africa. During the war and the peace conference, Nigerian newspapers such as the *Lagos Standard*, the *Times of Nigeria* and the *Nigerian Pioneer* frequently stated their support for Great Britain.[35] These papers repeatedly criticized German colonial policies and celebrated British military successes.[36] At the same time, they demanded recognition of the contribution African soldiers were making to the war effort.

At the war's end, the Nigerian press opposed Germany's

---

[34] "French Proposal for Partition of Togoland."

[35] Illustrations of these views can be found in "German Influence," *Lagos Standard*, December 9, 1914 and "Peace" *Nigerian Pioneer*, August 8, 1919, p. 6. Although the editor of the *Times of Nigeria*, James Bright Davies, had been sentenced to six months imprisonment for an article British colonial authorities viewed as seditious, his paper declared, "we have joined in prayer with the whole world... for the ultimate dismemberment of the German empire and for the total exclusion of Germany from ever holding hereafter any colonies in any portion of Africa." "The Great European War," October 24, 1916, p. 4. For a further discussion of Nigerian newspapers during the period see Fred I.A. Omu, *Press and Politics in Nigeria, 1880-1937* (London: Longman, 1978), pp. 211-221.

[36] Despite this elite support, among the general population in Nigeria there was widespread resistance to military service during the war. See James K. Matthews, "Reluctant Allies: Nigerian responses to military recruitment 1914-1918," *Africa and the First World War*, pp. 95-111.

return to Africa as a colonial power.[37] Yet the papers also
contained calls for the Allies to consult African wishes before
deciding the fate of Germany's former colonies. The *Lagos
Standard* stated its opinion that, "the British share in the disposal of the late German Colonies, without the previous consent of the peoples concerned, fills all Africans with painful
displeasure." The column recalled "the unratified promise of
the British Prime Minister to consult the native wishes" and
harshly attacked South African claims. "The rulers of South
Africa have not proved themsleves better than the Germans,
rather, they have, in the native view point, vied with them
with singular success in repressing the true owners of the land,
the Natives."[38]

The partition of West Africa likewise was denounced.

> Togoland is said to have been marked for France
> though it is too well known that the Togos, like
> the Cameroonians prefer British Government over
> and above any other.... It can cause them [the
> Great Powers] no pang, for Africans are theirs to
> be treated as they deem to their 'best interest.'
> Anglo-French interests must not clash and there-
> fore it were better Togoland be given to France
> quietly than run the risk of consulting the people
> whose bias is already only too well-known.[39]

---

[37] In the commercial field German firms often were compared favorably
with the British. Indeed, this is how Davies had aroused the ire of British
colonial authorities. See also "Future Relation with Germany," *Lagos Standard*, November 6, 1918.

[38] "The Late German Colonies," *Lagos Standard*, August 13, 1919. Until May 1919 the *Lagos Standard* had been edited by a leading African
nationalist, Geroge Williams. At the time of this article its editor was his
son, A.R. Williams.

[39] Ibid.

In the Gold Coast, the column signed "A Native of Aneho" continued to appear in the *Gold Coast Leader*. The author appealed to the Allied powers to apply in Africa the policies of self-determination and enlightened trusteeship. "The repartition of Africa is the topic of the hour.... The choice of such a change does not lie with an alien Power but with the people themselves," he wrote.[40]

Throughout 1919 his column demanded that African opinions should be sought on any redistribution of colonies. In March, he argued in an article titled "Neutralization and Internationalization of the Late German Colonies and the Voice of the People Concerned" that African preferences should be paramount. Continuing to emphasize this theme, articles in May appeared with the titles "The Principle of Self-Determination Applicable even in Moderate form to Africa," and "The Right of Togolanders to Choose their own Mandatory Power."[41]

The *Gold Coast Leader* argued that the people of Togo would favor a unified mandate under British administration, and the paper was not alone in adopting this position. One of the resolutions from the first meeting of the National Congress of British West Africa in 1920 called upon the European powers to respect African wishes in drawing colonial boundaries. In particular, this early pan-African group attacked the division of Togoland.[42] The weekly newspaper *Gold Coast Nation* – which differed with the editor of the *Gold Coast Leader*, Casely Hayford, on important issues – nevertheless adopted a similar attitude.[43] At Lomé, a Committee for Native Affairs

---

[40] "The Proposed Repartition of Africa," *Gold Coast Leader*, February 22, 1919, p. 4.

[41] *Gold Coast Leader*, March 15, 1919, p. 4; May 3-10, 1919, p. 4; and May 31-June 7, 1919, p. 4.

[42] David Kimble, *A Political History of Ghana* (Oxford: Clarendon Press, 1963), p. 384.

[43] See "The Future of Togoland," *Gold Coast Nation* , March 15, 1919, p. 2; along with "Future of the German Colonies," March 22-29, 1919, p. 3

was formed to oppose a French mandate for the colony. Octaviano Olympio, a leading member of the colony's black elite, reportedly served as president.[44]

These opinions did not represent the only viewpoints among Africans in Togo. The French produced statements of support in favor of their administration. At Lomé, the arrival of the steamer *Elmina* provoked a pro-German demonstration when it was mistaken for a return of the former colonial power. In at least the south of Togo, however, the desire for British administration did correspond with ethnic boundaries. The Ewe, who constituted the largest group in the area, had been divided by the Anglo-German colonial border. Assigning the area as a British mandate would have helped rectify this past colonial injustice.[45]

The strength of this argument was recognized by British officials. Hugh Clifford, the governor of the Gold Coast, cabled London:

> if principle of self determination is to be admitted whole occupied territory should be made British.... Cession of any portion of territory at present occupied by British Government will be fiercely resented by natives (of) concerned and would occasion great discontent among neighbouring tribes in Gold Coast and educated classes (of) throughout this Colony."[46]

---

and April 5, 1919, p. 5.

[44] "Togolanders, Demand For British Rule," *Gold Coast Leader*, July 26, 1919, pp. 3-4.

[45] See James Coleman, "Togoland," *International Conciliation*, No. 509, September 1956 (publication of the Carnegie Endowment for International Peace):8-9.

[46] Governor of the Gold Coast to the Secretary of State for the Colonies, telegram, March 4, 1919, FO 608/216/70142, PRO.

Yet in the end, British colonial decision makers disregarded these appeals and agreed to a division of Togo which favored France. Faced with the impending French mandate, "A Native of Aneho" wrote an article entitled "A Day of Sackcloth."[47]

The longer Cameroon border continued to be a matter of dispute.[48] As in Togo, the dominant topic of the discussions was the need to accommodate French plans to use the road traversing the area. The principal artery running north toward Chad paralleled and sometimes crossed the provisional Anglo-French division of the German colony.

Analyzing the Cameroon map presented by the French on May 20, Strachey commented:

> This road has been heavily inked in, in order to show that the French regard it as a ruling factor in the drawing of the boundary. They consider it essential that the whole length of the road should be in their territory.[49]

He acknowledged that the road was of more importance to the French and that they proposed to extend a railway along it. Consequently, he did not oppose British withdrawal from the portions which they held, but he believed the French should recognize that the British were making concessions.

In return for these concessions, Strachey hoped the French would accommodate British aims. In the north, he pointed out that the area was composed of small Islamic states with clear borders and that "it should be the rule to divide these units as rarely as possible." The most important of these was Bornu in

---

[47] *Gold Coast Leader*, August 30, 1919, pp. 3-4.

[48] My analysis here differs from Louis, *Great Britain and Germany's Lost Colonies*, p. 148. He observed that in comparison with Cameroon, "The Togoland negotiations were more acrimonious."

[49] "French Proposals for Partition of the Cameroons," C. Strachey, May 27, 1919, FO 608/215/70142, PRO.

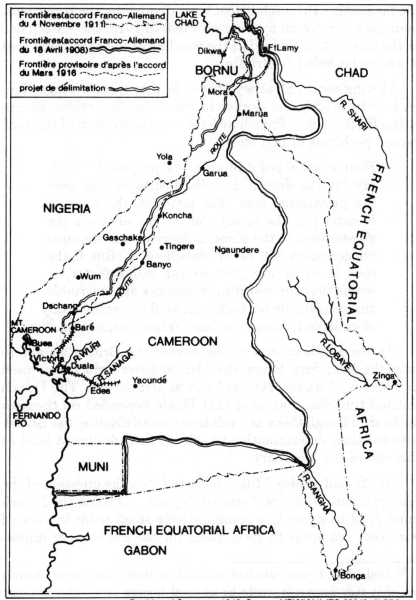

Partition of Cameroon 1919. Source: MPKK19(4) (FO 608/215),PRO.

182

the far north. Although it had been divided by the provisional
boundary line drawn by Georges Picot in 1916, the French had
at the time acknowledged in the wording of the agreement that
it was to be ceded to Britain.

Moving south, Strachey offered further specific suggestions
on how to modify the border to avoid dividing ethnic groups
in the British zone. French insistence on possession of the road
caused problems in this effort.

> From a tribal point of view, the proposed bound-
> ary [by the French] has disadvantages even over
> the provisional one. For instance, the town of
> Koncha (on the road) will be cut off from the
> greater part of the Koncha district, and the same
> phenomenon will occur elsewhere.... But if the
> road is to be accepted as the ruling factor, it
> seems that the resulting anomalies are inevitable
> and can only be partially palliated by careful study
> of local conditions by a delimitation commission.[50]

At the southern end of the border the British sought to
have the boundary follow the Mungo River, which was used
as a means of transportation by local plantations. The French
resisted this claim, arguing that Duala depended on the area
for food. Though this was a relatively small dispute, the British
asserted their determination to achieve their desires at least at
this end of the boundary.

At the end of May Milner observed, "on the question of the
Mungo mouth I am not disposed to yield....I think the French
must yield to us on this comparatively small point in view of
our great readiness to meet them on the much more impor-

---

[50] Ibid. The French also had included on their map a water-parting
line that they suggested would be an ideal frontier, but which Strachey
generally viewed as a device aimed at convincing the British that they were
being "dealt with generously."

tant issue of the road."[51] Two weeks later, continuing French reluctance to concede this and other matters led Strachey to remark: "At Lord Milner's first meeting with M. Simon, it was understood that our friends were prepared to be very accommodating over the Cameroons boundary, but, I confess that I do not find many signs of this in their proposals."[52]

Finally, at a meeting on June 28 Simon conceded the Mungo to the British. Milner and Simon now were able to sign a declaration of boundary recommendations for Cameroon and Togo. This London agreement of July 10 did not, however, represent a conclusive settlement on the future of Cameroon and Togo.

The French Colonial Ministry refused to give up the prerogative of raising troops and at first even was unwilling to acknowledge that the French sections of Cameroon and Togo were held under a mandate. In a conversation with President Poincaré on May 16, Simon reportedly asserted that before the Council of Four "he had insisted that we should have Cameroon and the Congo [Simon's reference may be to the territories lost in 1911, or he may have meant Togo.], without mandate and directly."[53] Despite this affirmation, Poincaré described Simon as unsure how the Council of Four's decision on May 7 should be interpreted. According to Simon the accord would be " 'recommendated' [sic] to the League of Nations" but he didn't know whether this was to be translated "recommended, communicated or submitted."[54]

---

[51] Minute signed: M. 30.5.19, on Strachey memorandum "Partition of the Cameroons," May 29, 1919, FO 608/215/70142, PRO.

[52] "Cameroons. Notes on French proposals." The record of meeting of June 13th, 1919, FO 608/215/70142, PRO.

[53] Raymond Poincaré, *Au service de la France*, 11 vols. *A la recherche de la paix, 1919*, preface by Pierre Renouvin, notes by Jacques Bariéty and Pierre Miquel, published posthumously from his unedited papers (Paris: Librairie Plon, 1928-69), 11:431.

[54] Ibid.

On May 29, Milner wrote Simon that according to Lloyd
George the question of applying mandates had been reserved
for the moment. Consequently, Milner believed that the two
ministers should restrict their recommendations to the delimitation of boundaries.[55] In an internal British memorandum,
Milner stated that both Britain and France agreed that mandates should not be applied to their spheres of Togo, which
ought to be incorporated into the neighboring colonies. Considerations surrounding Cameroon, he thought, were more complicated. These included the question, "Why should France
receive the German Cameroons in full sovereignty, while Great
Britain receives German East Africa under a mandate?"[56]

On June 27, the Council of Four appointed the Commission
on Colonial Mandates and charged it with drafting the mandates and examining Belgian and Portuguese claims in German
East Africa. Conflicting views soon surfaced. At the second
meeting of the commission, debate broke out over French proposals permitting compulsory military service and the use of
troops from the mandate to defend metropolitan France. Simon maintained that this had been agreed to on January 30.[57]
Beer and Cecil, a strong supporter of the League, objected
to this interpretation and initiated a debate which continued
the following day. Colonel House even argued that the French
position could threaten American approval of the peace treaty.

Unable to resolve the dispute, the delegates turned to other
matters and soon found themselves involved in another clash
of interests. During the fourth meeting of the commission, the
question of guaranteeing economic equality in the mandates

---

[55] Milner to Simon, May 29, 1919, Milner Papers, 389:132, BLO.

[56] "Cameroons and Togoland," Milner, May 29, 1919, Milner Papers,
389:140-143.

[57] "Notes of the Second Meeting of the Commission on Mandates, July
8, 1919." File No. 181.227, General Records of the America Commission to
Negotiate Peace, NA.

was discussed. Simon took the position that on important public works, such as telegraph lines, foreign competition could be avoided. He "considered that it would be most unfair that all the benefits of occupation under the Mandate go to foreigners and all the cost to the Mandatory Power."[58]

House argued that the French position violated the principle of economic equality within the mandates. In addition, Beer pointed out that the beneficiaries of competitive bidding would be the inhabitants of the mandatory territories. Yet it is equally apparent that the result of the American position would be to protect the economic interests of the United States.

At the end of August, Strachey wrote that what had been accomplished was but the first step. The form of the mandates, and even whether one would be applied to Togo, still remained to be settled.[59] In the face of Anglo-American opposition, the French continued to maintain that they had the right to raise troops. Final agreement on the form of the B mandates required extensive further negotiations, and the mandates were not confirmed by the League of Nations until July 1922.[60]

---

[58] "Notes of the Fourth Meeting of the Commission on Mandates, July 9, 1919," ibid.

[59] "Future Division of Togoland & Cameroons between British & French authority," printed note, C. Strachey, August 29, 1919, FO 608/215/70412, PRO.

[60] For a detailed discussion of these subsequent developments see Andrew J. Crozier, "The Establishment of the Mandates System 1919-25," *Journal of Contemporary History* 14 (1979):483-513, Hessel Duncan Hall, *Mandates, Dependencies and Trusteeship* (Washington, D.C.: Carnegie Endowment for International Peace, 1948), pp. 134-154 and Quincy Wright, *Mandates under the League of Nations* (Chicago: University of Chicago Press, 1930), pp. 43-45 and 52-56.

East Africa

Constructing an imperialist settlement in this part of the continent proved an even more controversial task than in Cameroon and Togo. Britain, which lacking essential interests in the West had been willing to make concessions there, approached German East Africa with a different attitude. The dominant role of troops from the British Empire in the conquest of the colony, its strategic importance for communications and defense, its commercial potential and Britain's greater apprehension over native interests dictated a less accommodating policy.

At the same time, Belgian negotiators tenaciously defended their perceived colonial rights, while hoping to arrange a large-scale exchange of African territory.[61] They may have held an exaggerated view of the military contribution in East Africa made by soldiers from the Belgian Congo. Yet they were not amiss in realizing that their occupation of East African territory gave them an object of value for which the British would have to negotiate. The colonial expert Pierre Orts was entrusted with the principal responsibility for these talks and was assisted by Octave Louwers. In early March, Milner sought a

---

[61] In this regard the Belgian delegation was more zealous than Colonial Minister Franck. Foreign Minister Hymans wrote to him that he did not place great enough emphasis upon acquiring the left bank of the Congo. Hymans continued, "In my opinion, the acquisition of the left bank of the Congo is of the first importance. It must be placed among the principal preoccupations of Belgium." Hymans to Franck, February 5, 1919, Paris, Af 1/2 8743, AMAE,B. Later, Franck suggested to Hymans that abandoning Ruanda would not cause any inconvenience to Belgium, an observation which brought an astonished reply from Octave Louwers, who viewed the region as having an "inestimable richness, and one does not understand how a colonial minister so easily envisions abandoning it." Louwers note, conversation with Hymans on March 8, 1919, Af 1/4, "Sort de l'Est Africain/Accords Orts-Milner," dossier I, January-October 1919, AMAE,B.

meeting with a Belgian representative to exchange views on territorial questions in Africa. The Belgians were reluctant to have anyone but Orts conduct these talks, and consequently, with first Orts and then Milner away from Paris, a meeting was not arranged until March 20.[62] Milner told Orts that the reason he wanted to see him was to settle African questions, particularly those related to German East Africa. Milner believed it would be best to settle these issues themselves and then submit their agreement to the conference, where he was convinced it would be accepted. Orts hastened to concur.[63]

When they met again that afternoon both claimed the disputed areas of East Africa, but Orts seemed hopeful. He believed a deal could be struck by which Belgium would retain Ruanda while ceding a passage west of Lake Victoria to the English. Britain, in turn, was expected to assist Belgium in its efforts to acquire the left bank of the Congo and Cabinda from Portugal.[64] Although negotiations did not progress further until mid-May, Orts's program was an accurate outline of the direction they were to follow.

As in the case of West Africa, discussions resumed after the decisions of the Council of Four. On May 12 and 14, Orts and Milner held long discussions. Orts initially sought to overturn the decision allocating German East Africa only to Britain, but faced with Milner's opposition he abandoned this demand. According to Milner,

> The line which M. Orts took in subsequent
> discussion was simply this, that Belgium had taken
> part (an important part as he contended) in the

---

[62] Strachey to Louwers, March 5, 1919, Paris; Louwers to Orts, March 7, 1919, Paris; Strachey to Louwers, March 12, 1919, Paris, Af 1/2 8782, 8785, 8789, AMAE,B.

[63] Louwers memorandum, n.d., Af 1/2 8800, AMAE,B.

[64] "Conclusions à tirer de notre entretien avec Lord Milner, le 20 mars 1919," Orts note, Af 1/2 8802 and Louis, *Ruanda-Urundi*, pp. 235-236.

conquest of German East Africa; that as a consequence of her military effort she was and had
been for three years past, in the occupation of a
portion of that country which, though of considerable extent, was only a small proportion of the
whole; and that it was only fair she should be allowed to retain this portion, as we were retaining
the much more extensive part now in our occupation. My reply to this was, that I could not
admit that the conquest of any particular portion of enemy territory constituted a claim to the
mandate for that territory, and that the whole
question must be looked at from a much broader
point of view.[65]

Milner then argued that on both geographic and ethnic
grounds Belgian retention of any large part of German East
Africa did not make sense. Beyond these objections, he "emphatically" pointed out that there were certain areas which
Britain "could not possibly agree to their retaining." These
were control of the western end of the central railroad and a corridor of territory west of Lake Victoria through which Britain
could in the future construct a north-south railway line.

Here the British disregarded African interests to fulfill the
imperialist dream of the Cape-to-Cairo railway. Britain insisted on retaining territory west of the Kagera River, although
the river was generally recognized as Ruanda's eastern boundary.[66]

After further sparring, Orts sent Milner an official proposal
on May 19, essentially accepting Britain's nonnegotiable de-

---

[65] "Negotiations with Belgium about German East Africa," Milner Memorandum, Milner Papers 389:156-182, BLO.

[66] Continuing discontent in Ruanda over this act led to a reversal of the
decision in 1923. The area west of the Kagera River was then placed under
the Belgian mandate, reuniting Ruanda's territory.

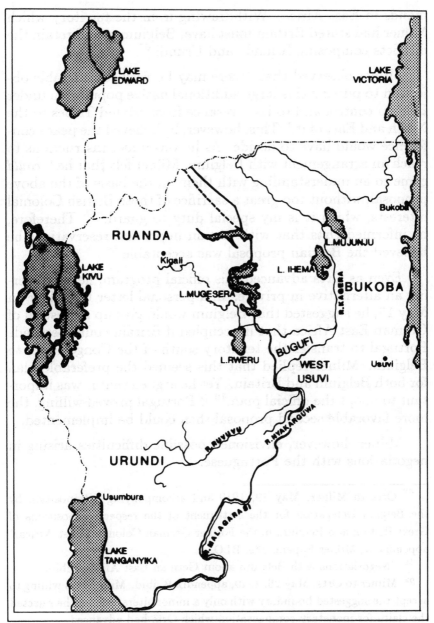

Ruanda Urundi Source: MPK 272(1) (FO 608/216).PRO.

mands in East Africa. Withdrawing from the territory which Milner had stated Britain must have, Belgium would retain the districts composing Ruanda and Urundi.[67]

Milner observed that "there may be very considerable objection to putting this large additional native population under Belgian control and to its severance from related Tribes to the North and East of it." This, however, he believed the peace conference would have to decide. As he was under instructions to reach an arrangement with Belgium, Milner felt that he " *could* come to an understanding with them on the basis of the above proposal, without too great a sacrifice of those British Colonial interests, which it is my special duty to guard."[68] Therefore, he informed Orts that with certain important reservations he believed the Belgian proposal was acceptable.[69]

Even as Orts advanced this official program, he was offering an alternative in private. In a personal letter to Milner on May 19, he suggested that Belgium would give up almost all of German East Africa that it occupied if Britain could persuade Portugal to transfer the territory south of the Congo River to Belgium. Milner replied that this seemed the preferable plan for both Belgium and Britain. Yet he argued that it was important to adopt the official plan.[70] If Portugal proved willing, the more favorable second proposal then could be implemented.

Milner, however, envisioned possible difficulties arising in negotiations with the Portuguese.

---

[67] Orts to Milner, May 19, 1919 and accompanying "Proposition by the Belgian Delegation for the settlement of the respective positions of Great Britain and Belgium in the Former German Colony of East Africa," appendix A, Milner Papers, 389, BLO.

[68] "Negotiations with Belgium about German East Africa," ibid.

[69] Milner to Orts, May 26, 1919, appendix B, ibid. Milner was willing to accept the suggested boundary with only a minor alteration, but he rejected the claim for monetary compensation which Orts had advanced.

[70] Milner to Orts, private, May 26, 1919, appendix C, ibid.

> If we ask the Portuguese to give up the terri-
> tory which you want South of the Congo mouth,
> they will certainly look for territorial compensa-
> tion. It is not easy to see, where such territorial
> compensation can be found. It may be possible –
> there are many difficulties but these may not be
> insuperable – to find it in the South Eastern cor-
> ner of German East Africa, between the Rovuma
> and the Mbemkuro. But even if the Portuguese
> accepted the cession of territory to them in this
> quarter in exchange for what you wish to obtain
> from them near the Congo mouth, I can see that
> we should have to encounter considerable opposi-
> tion to the proposal to hand over any fresh native
> population to the Portuguese.[71]

On May 30 Milner and Orts agreed to submit the official plan to the Council of Four. Responding to a personal
letter from Lord Charles Hindlip, Milner succinctly described
the stage of discussions at this point and provided an illustrative summary of the British negotiating position. Milner
observed that he had entered the discussions "with not quite a
free hand." "We had practically committed ourselves to giving
the Belgians something, and there is no denying that they have
some claim."

Although the Belgians would retain Ruanda and Urundi,
Milner pointed out that:

> ... they will retire from the whole of the Central
> railway line between Dar-es-Salam and Ujiji, of
> which they at present hold the western end, and
> also leave us a broad extent of territory west of
> Lake Nyanza, which will give us uninterrupted
> railway connection with Uganda.

---

[71] Ibid.

As for the territory the Belgians retained, Milner continued:

> Of course I should have preferred to keep this, as I understand it is a good cattle country with a large native population, and it is possible that, as a result of some further negotiations with the Belgians and the Portuguese, we may be able to get the Belgians even out of this.

He concluded that allowing the Belgians to keep Ruanda and Urundi was not an "ideal" solution but the "best of which the circumstances at present permit."[72]

The "preferable" imperialist exchange of territories foundered, however, upon Portugal's adamant refusal to surrender any portion of its possessions. This position had been stated clearly by the Portuguese in March and April during conversations with Louwers.

On March 19, Louwers had met with Alfredo Freire d'Andrade, the Portuguese adviser on colonial questions, at the Hotel Campbell in Paris. D'Andrade promised that favorable arrangements could be made for Belgian interests in the Bas-Congo, including communications with the sea and transit and telegraph lines. Yet he warned that Portuguese public opinion must be considered. "Our public opinion, which does not even know the location of all of our colonies, is extremely sensitive on the subject of the integrity of our colonial domain," cautioned d'Andrade.[73]

---

[72] Milner to Hindlip, June 10, 1919, MSS English History, C. 704:418-419, BLO. Hindlip served in South Africa during the Boer War and from 1907 to 1914 was junior Unionist Whip in the House of Lords. He had traveled extensively in Africa and was involved with a variety of British business enterprises in East Africa.

[73] Louwers memorandum, March 19, 1919, Paris, Af 1/2 8796, AMAE,B.

These views were repeated when the two men met again. Knowledge of Belgian colonial aims had upset the Portuguese. According to d'Andrade,

> M. Costa [the former Portuguese premier and the Portuguese representative to the peace conference] has declared that he would never consent to abandoning the smallest piece of our colonial domain. Lord Milner has just talked with us on the same question. He spoke to M. Costa of your aspirations in enlarging the Belgian Congo's access to the sea. All of this is not taking place without creating a very unfavorable impression on the Portuguese delegation.[74]

D'Andrade had sought the present meeting to find out just what the Belgians wanted and to see if there was a way to satisfy their desires. Transportation facilities, such as the construction of a new port at Kissinga connected by a railway to Belgian territory, he suggested might be arranged. Louwers, however, outlined in vague language the possibility of the three-way exchange with Britain and added that the Portuguese were proposing a solution which gave the Belgians "the advantages of sovereignty, but without sovereignty." Such a solution he thought the Belgian government would not accept.

D'Andrade replied that although in the future colonial territory might be exchanged for needed funding, at the moment it was not possible. "If one spoke of this in our country, he would be stoned to death; but at a time in the future, in two or three years,... then you can obtain satisfaction."[75] Thus, the partition of German East Africa agreed to by Orts and Milner endured.

---

[74] Louwers memorandum, April 4, 1919, Af 1/2 8811, AMAE,B.
[75] Ibid.

194

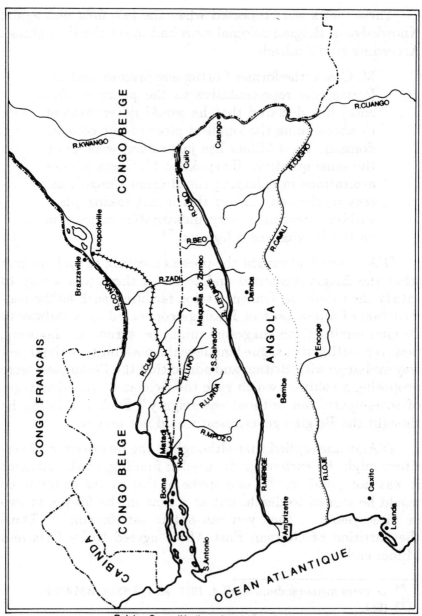

Belgian Congo/Northern Angola Source: Milner Papers 389:126,BLO.

The Portuguese had hoped to be allotted a mandate in the southern part of German East Africa quite apart from negotiations with the Belgians. This claim was rejected scornfully by the British, who deprecated the Portuguese military effort and criticized their colonial practices. During von Lettow-Vorbeck's invasion of northern Mozambique leaders of the Makua had shifted their loyalty to the Germans, and the Portuguese took harsh reprisals.[76] British criticism contained an element of hypocrisy, however, as Britain would have ceded territory to Portugal in the three-way trade involving Belgium. In the end, Portugal was granted outright a small section of territory south of the Rovuma River, known as the Kionga Triangle.[77]

There remained a final hurdle before the Anglo-Belgian partition of German East Africa gained the same peace conference and League approval as the partition of Togo and Cameroon. Before the Commission on Colonial Mandates, Baron de Gaiffier presented the Orts-Milner agreement of May 30. Beer alone objected, pointing out that these territories differed from the Belgian Congo on ethnic, economic and political grounds as well as being geographically isolated from the Belgian colony.[78]

In the privacy of his diary, Beer elaborated more explicitly upon his objections.

> This agreement cannot be defended except on grounds of merest expediency. It is contrary to

---

[76] Malyn Newitt, *Portugal in Africa: The Last Hundred Years* (London: Longman, 1981), p. 63.

[77] See Milner, "Postscript Memorandum on Negotiations with Belgium," May 29, 1919, Milner Papers 389:181-182 and General Van Deventer, Dar-es-Salaam, to the War Office, June 25, 1918 and July 7, 1918, Milner Papers 363:379-383, BLO.

[78] "Report made by the Commission on Belgian claims in East Africa," July 17, 1919, Commission on Colonial Mandates, file no. 181.227, General Records of the American Commission to Negotiate Peace, NA.

> the fundamental principles upon which these colo-
> nies were to be disposed of in that no attention
> at all was paid to native interests.... England,
> as Amery said, did not want to appear greedy as
> regards a small nation like Belgium.[79]

Although Beer's protest found no higher proponent and the United States acquiesced in the settlement, the criticism remains poignant. The British were well aware of its validity.

When Orts informed Milner that the Belgians had received a large number of African requests that they extend their rule into Ruanda and Urundi, Milner asked his experts about the assertion's accuracy. Major E.S. Grogan, who had served in East Africa during the war, responded: "No natives in all Central Africa would on their own initiative do anything of the kind."[80]

Imperialism's New Clothes

The foregoing investigation of Allied colonial objectives in tropical Africa reveals no monocausal motivation. Wartime animosity and the ancient belief that the spoils of war belong to the victor accounted for the decision to confiscate Germany's colonies. African interests, proclaimed in public as the basis of Allied policy, were largely disregarded in private. Instead, the repartition of tropical Africa conformed to the differing colonial ambitions of the European states. Wartime developments produced new incentives, but over all there existed a strong continuity with past aims.

In West Africa, the French desire to improve access to their colonies in the interior of the continent, coupled with

---

[79] "Belgian Claims," Paris, July 13 to August 4, Beer, Manuscript Diary, p. 136.

[80] Detailed Grogan minute (June 5) on a confidential note from H.C. Thornton, June 4, 1919, MSS English History, C. 704:358, BLO.

Anglo-French recognition of France's right to compensation for Britain's other colonial gains, were the decisive factors in determining the partition of Cameroon and Togo. Time and again throughout the war, French colonial officials had emphasized the value of the two colonies as natural outlets to the Atlantic for the African hinterland they controlled. At the peace conference, this proved the most important determinant in drawing the mandate boundaries.

British decision makers believed their interests in the area were secondary to colonial objectives elsewhere. From the outset of the war, they placed a higher priority on excluding their allies from German East Africa. Among the most important reasons for this British policy was the traditional interest in controlling the route to India, Australia and New Zealand. Submarine warfare, combined with the *Königsberg* episode, provided a new dimension to this long-standing concern.

British objectives also were influenced by revival of the Cape-to-Cairo railway scheme. The German colony represented the remaining obstacle to a line of contiguous British possessions stretching from South Africa to Egypt. Although many British policy makers viewed the railroad plan as impractical, they were unable to resist its geographic appeal.

Belgian colonial aims reflected the anxieties of a small state. Initially fearful that the Belgian Congo might be sacrificed in a compromise peace, Belgian officials later viewed offensive operations against German East Africa as a means for restoring their image in African eyes while assuring themselves colonial bargaining chips at the peace conference. With regard to colonial territorial acquisitions, their leading priority was increasing their colony's access to the Atlantic. This policy they pursued with perhaps the most brazen self-interest exhibited in any of the negotiations over the German colonies.

Almost uniformly, Colonial Ministry officials in each of the three countries supported policies of territorial expansion. They both advanced and justified the addition of new provinces to their empires. Louis Franck, Belgium's colonial minister during the peace conference, was clearly atypical among Colonial Ministry officials in urging his government to pursue a moderate policy.

The comparative strength of economic motives during the war is hard to evaluate. Security concerns naturally assumed a more prominent position than they would have during peace time. Still, specific studies of the economic potential of the German colonies were undertaken and characteristically provided favorable assessments.[81] Even more general Allied position papers normally anticipated that their metropolitan industries would benefit from the raw materials and new markets to be found in the territories.

Of all the arguments advanced by the Allies, the claim of protecting African interests was the most self-serving and sophistical, despite the fact that the creation of the mandate system and the corresponding involvement of the United States did moderate the tone of imperialism.

The hypocrisy of the Allied position clearly manifested itself in attitudes toward the future training and use of African soldiers from the former German colonies. German colonialism was denounced for militarizing Africa. But the French insisted more tenaciously on the right to raise troops in Togo and Cameroon than on any other point in the mandate system.

If the Anglo-American opposition to this French stand appears more enlightened, it should be recognized that the British position coincided with a well-established objective of the Union of South Africa. The widespread use of African troops during the war had thoroughly alarmed Pretoria. The white minority government feared that the training of black soldiers in Africa

---

[81] For example, see "British Trade Interests in the German Overseas Possessions," T.C. 15, Board of Trade, October 10, 1916, CAB 16/36/66737, PRO.

could force South Africa to follow the same policy and thereby weaken white hegemony.

Allied leaders also argued that their confiscation and division of the German colonies corresponded with African wishes. In part, this justification represented the unfeigned confidence of Allied officials in the superiority of their colonial administrations. Yet, Allied leaders and colonial officials were aware that they were manufacturing many of the African statements of preference for their rule which they produced in public. This was particularly true of British policy makers, who placed the greatest emphasis on the issue.

A more genuine collection of African opinions also exists. Whether gleaned from African newspapers and statements or from the field reports of British officials, African views that were frequently in conflict with the decisions reached in Paris can be identified. African voices were not completely silent; their rhetoric aside, the colonial powers were not listening. In the end, despite attempts to cloak Allied aims in altruistic terms, inter-Allied rivalry produced a division of Germany's tropical African colonies that reflected not African desires but European colonial priorities.

Selected Bibliography

Manuscript Sources

Belgium

Archives Générales du Royaume, Brussels
    Jules van den Heuvel Papers
    Pierre Orts Papers
        Politique coloniale et revendications coloniales
        1916-1919

Archives du Ministère des Affaires Etrangères, Brussels
    Collection Afrique
        Af 1/2: Guerre 1914-1918
        Af 1/3: Congo guerre
        Af 1/4: Sort de l'Est Africain;
            Accords Orts-Milner

France

Archives du Ministère des Affaires Etrangères, Paris
    Série A: Conférence de la Paix, 1914-1920
        78: Colonies allemandes 1917-1920
    Série Afrique: 1918-1940
    Série Guerre: 1914-1918
        1544: Possessions allemandes d'Afrique I
        1545: Possessions allemandes d'Afrique II
            Opérations militaires franco-
            britanniques, 1914 août-décembre
        1553: Congo Belge

1562: Possessions anglaises d'Afrique Orientale
Tardieu Papers
Doumergue Papers

Archives Nationales, Section Outre-Mer, Paris
    Fonds Affaires Politiques
        3254: Commission de documentation
          97: Procès-verbaux de la commission
              d'études des questions coloniales
              posées par la guerre
        1044: Programme de paix. Détermination du
              sort réservé aux colonies allemandes et
              préparation des formules des mandats
    Séries Géographiques
        Afrique IV expansion territorial
        71: Colonies allemandes 1912-1916

Great Britain

Bodleian Library, Oxford
    Harcourt Papers
    Milner Papers
    MSS English History (Additional Milner Papers)

House of Lords Record Office, London
    Bonar Law Papers
    Davidson Papers
    Lloyd George Papers

Public Record Office, Kew
    Cabinet Papers
        CAB 16/36: Committee of Imperial Defence.
                   Sub-Committee on Territorial
                   Changes

CAB 21/77: Imperial War Cabinet.
Committee to Consider the
Territorial Desiderata in the
Terms of Peace
CAB 23: War Cabinet Minutes
CAB 24: Cabinet. Memoranda
CAB 29/1: Committee of Imperial Defence.
Peace Papers
CAB 29/9: British War Cabinet.
Paris Peace Conference
Colonial Office Papers
691: Tanganyika: Original Correspondence
Foreign Office Papers
371: General Correspondence: Political
Africa (War)
608: Peace Conference of 1919 to 1920:
Correspondence

United States

Library of Congress, Washington, D.C.
George Louis Beer's Diary

National Archives, Washington, D.C.
General Records of the American Commission to
Negotiate Peace 1918-1931

Government Documents

Belgium, Ministère des Affaires Etrangères. *Diplomatic Correspondence respecting the War*. London: His Majesty's Stationery Office, 1914.

Great Britain. Parliament. *Parliamentary Debates* (Commons). 5th series. Vol. 100, 1917.

United States, Department of State. *Papers Relating to the Foreign Relations of the United States: The Paris Peace Conference, 1919.* Vols. 3 and 5. Washington, D.C.: Government Printing Office, 1943-44.

_____. *Papers Relating to the Foreign Relations of the United States: The World War.* Supplement 1. Washington, D.C.: Government Printing Office, 1931.

Contemporary Journals and Newspapers

L'Afrique Française

Gold Coast Leader

Journal of the African Society

Lagos Standard

The Round Table

Books and Unpublished Dissertations

Andrew, C.M. and Kanya-Forstner, A.S. *The Climax of French Imperial Expansion, 1914-1924.* Stanford: Stanford University Press, 1981.

Antonelli, Etienne. *L'Afrique et la paix de Versailles.* Paris: B. Grasset, 1921.

Austen, Ralph A. *Northwest Tanzania under German and British Rule.* New Haven: Yale University Press, 1968.

Barton, Frank. *The Press of Africa: Persecution and Perseverance.* London: Macmillan Press, 1979.

Baumgart, Winfried. *Imperialism: The Idea and Reality of British and French Colonial Expansion, 1880-1914.* Oxford: Oxford University Press, 1982.

Beer, George Louis. *African Questions at the Paris Peace Conference.* New York: Macmillan Co., 1923.

George Louis Beer: A Tribute to His Life and Work in the Making of History and the Moulding of Public Opinion. New York: Macmillan Co., 1924.

Birdsall, Paul. *Versailles Twenty Years After.* New York: Reynal and Hitchcock, 1941.

Boahen, A. Adu, ed. *Unesco General History of Africa: Africa under Colonial Domination 1880-1935.* Vol. 7. Berkeley and Los Angeles: University of California Press, 1985.

Brown, J.M. "War and the Colonial Relationship: Britain, India and the War of 1914-1918." *War and Society: Historical Essays in Honour and Memory of J.R. Western.* Edited by Michael Foot. London: Elek, 1973.

Brunschwig, Henri. *L'expansion allemande outre-mer du XVe siècle à nos jours.* Paris: Presses universitaires de France, 1957.

Cobban, Alfred. *The Nation State and National Self-Determination.* New York: Thomas Y. Crowell Co., 1970.

‒‒‒‒‒‒‒‒. *National Self-Determination.* London: Oxford University Press, 1948.

Collins, Robert O. "The Origins of the Nile Struggle: Anglo-German Negotiations and the Mackinnon Agreement of 1890." In *Britain and Germany in Africa: Imperial Rivalry and Colonial Rule.* Edited by Prosser Gifford and William Roger Louis. New Haven: Yale University Press, 1967.

Cooke, James J. *New French Imperialism 1880-1910: The Third Republic and Colonial Expansion.* Hamden, Conn.: Archon Books, 1973.

Cookey, S.J.S. *Britain and the Congo Question, 1885-1913.* London: Longmans, Green and Co., 1968.

Coquery-Vidrovitch, Catherine. "French Colonization in Africa to 1920: Administration and Economic Development." In *Colonialism in Africa 1870-1960*. Vol. 1. *The History and Politics of Colonialism 1870-1914*. Edited by L.H. Gann and Peter Duignan. Cambridge: Cambridge University Press, 1969.

Corbett, Sir Julian S. *History of the Great War: Naval Operations*. Vol. 3. London: Longmans, Green and Co., 1923.

Crowder, Michael. "The 1914-1918 European War and West Africa." *History of West Africa*. Vol. 2. Edited by J.F.A. Ajayi and M. Crowder. London: Longman Group, 1974.

Dundas, Sir Charles. *African Crossroads*. London: Macmillan and Co., 1955.

Egerton, George W. *Great Britain and the Creation of the League of Nations: Strategy, Politics, and International Organization, 1914-1919*. Chapel Hill: University of North Carolina Press, 1978.

Farwell, Byron. *The Great War in Africa, 1914-1918*. New York: W.W. Norton and Co., 1986.

Fidel, Camille. *La paix coloniale française*. Paris: L. Tenin, 1918.

First, Ruth. *South West Africa*. Baltimore: Penguin Books, 1963.

Fischer, Fritz. *Germany's Aims in the First World War*. New York: W.W. Norton and Co., 1967.

_____. *War of Illusions: German Policies from 1911 to 1914*. Translated by Marian Jackson. New York: W.W. Norton and Co., 1975.

Gann, L.H. and Duignan, Peter. *The Rulers of British Africa 1870-1914*. Stanford: Stanford University Press, 1978.

_____. *The Rulers of German Africa 1884-1914.* Stanford: Stanford University Press, 1977.

Gatzke, Hans. *Germany's Drive to the West.* Baltimore: Johns Hopkins Press, 1950.

Gelfand, Lawrence E. *The Inquiry: American Preparations for Peace, 1917-1919.* New Haven: Yale University Press, 1963.

Georges, Brigadier General E. Howard. *The Great War in West Africa.* London: Hutchinson and Co., 1930.

Gollin, Alfred M. *Proconsul in Politics: A Study of Lord Milner in Opposition and in Power.* London: A. Blond, 1964.

Guinn, Paul. *British Strategy and Politics, 1914 to 1918.* Oxford: Clarendon Press, 1965.

Gupta, Partha. *Imperialism and the British Labour Movement, 1914-1964.* New York: Holmes and Meier Publishers, 1975.

Hachten, William A. *Muffled Drums: The News Media in Africa.* Ames: Iowa State University Press, 1971.

Hall, Hessel Duncan. "The British Commonwealth and the Founding of the League Mandate System." *Studies in International History.* Edited by K. Bourne and D.C. Watt. Hamden, Conn.: Archon Books, 1967.

_____. *Mandates, Dependencies and Trusteeship.* Washington, D.C.: Carnegie Endowment for International Peace, 1948.

Hankey, Sir Maurice. *The Supreme Control at the Paris Peace Conference 1919: A Commentary.* London: Allen Unwin, 1963.

Hargreaves, John D. "British and French Imperialism in West Africa, 1885-1898." In *France and Britain in Africa: Imperial Rivalry and Colonial Rule.* Edited by Prosser

Gifford and William Roger Louis. New Haven: Yale University Press, 1971.

Hawkin, R.C. "The Belgian Proposal to Neutralise Central Africa during the European War." *Problems of the War: Papers read before the Grotius Society in the Year 1915.* Vol. 1. London: Sweet and Maxell, 1916.

Heisser, David. "The Impact of the Great War on French Imperialism, 1914-1924." Ph.D. Thesis: University of North Carolina, Chapel Hill, 1972.

Helmreich, Jonathan E. *Belgium and Europe: A Study in Small Power Diplomacy.* The Hague: Mouton, 1976.

Henderson, William O. *Studies in German Colonial History.* Chicago: Quadrangle Books, 1962.

Hodges, Geoffrey. *The Carrier Corps: Military Labor in the East African Campaign, 1914-1918.* New York: Greenwood Press, 1986.

Hogben, S.J. and Kirk-Greene, A.H.M. *The Emirates of Northern Nigeria.* London: Oxford University Press, 1966.

Hordern, Lieutenant-Colonel Charles. *Official History of the War: Military Operations East Africa.* Vol. 1. London: His Majesty's Stationery Office, 1941.

Hyam, Ronald. *The Failure of South African Expansion, 1908-1948.* London: Macmillan, 1972.

Hynes, William G. *The Economics of Empire: Britain, Africa and the New Imperialism 1879-95.* London: Longman Group, 1979.

Iliffe, John. *Tanganyika Under German Rule.* Cambridge: Cambridge University Press, 1969.

Ingham, Kenneth. *A History of East Africa.* Revised Edition. New York: Frederick A. Praeger, 1965.

Kaspi, André. "French War Aims in Africa, 1914-1919." In *France and Britain in Africa: Imperial Rivalry and Colonial Rule*. Edited by Prosser Gifford and William Roger Louis. New Haven: Yale University Press, 1971.

Kimble, David. *A Political History of Ghana: The Rise of Gold Coast Nationalism, 1850-1928*. Oxford: Clarendon Press, 1963.

Kirk-Greene, A.H.M. *Adamawa: Past and Present*. London: Oxford University Press, 1958.

Knoll, Arthur J. *Togo Under Imperial Germany 1884-1914*. Stanford: Hoover Institution Press, 1978.

Lansing, Robert. *The Peace Negotiations*. Boston: Houghton Mifflin, 1921.

Lettow-Vorbeck, General Paul von. *My Reminiscences of East Africa*. London: Hurst and Blackett, 1920.

Le Vine, Victor. *The Cameroons from Mandate to Independence*. Berkeley and Los Angeles: University of California Press, 1964.

Link, Arthur S. *Wilson the Diplomatist*. Baltimore: Johns Hopkins Press, 1957; reprint edition, New York: New Viewpoints, 1974.

Lloyd George, David. *War Memoirs of David Lloyd George*. 2 vols. London: Odhams Press, 1942.

_____. *The Truth about the Peace Treaties*. 2 vols. London: Victor Gollancz, 1938.

Louis, William Roger. "Great Britain and German Expansion in Africa, 1884-1919." In *Britain and Germany in Africa: Imperial Rivalry and Colonial Rule*. Edited by Prosser Gifford and William Roger Louis. New Haven: Yale University Press, 1967.

_____. *Great Britain and Germany's Lost Colonies 1914-1919*. Oxford: Clarendon Press, 1967.

_____. *Ruanda-Urundi 1884-1919*. Oxford: Clarendon Press, 1963.

Mangin, Lieutenant-Colonel Charles. *La Force noire*. Paris: Librairie Hachette, 1911.

Mansergh, Nicholas. *The Commonwealth Experience*. Vol. 1. Revised edition. Toronto: University of Toronto Press, 1983.

Mantoux, Paul. *Les délibérations du conseil des quatre*. 2 vols. Paris: Éditions du centre national de la recherche scientifique, 1955.

Marks, Sally. *Innocent Abroad: Belgium at the Paris Peace Conference of 1919*. Chapel Hill: University of North Carolina Press, 1981.

Marston, F.S. *The Peace Conference of 1919, Organization and Procedure*. New York: Frank Swain, 1944.

Martet, Jean, ed. *M. Clemenceau peint par lui-même*. Paris: A. Michel, 1929.

Martin, Laurence W. *Peace without Victory: Woodrow Wilson and the British Liberals*. Port Washington, N.Y.: Kennikat Press, 1973.

Mayer, Arno J. *Political Origins of the New Diplomacy, 1917-1918*. New York: Howard Fertig, 1969.

_____. *Politics and Diplomacy of Peacemaking, 1918-1919*. New York: Alfred A. Knopf, 1967.

Michel, Marc. *L'Appel à l'Afrique: Contributions et réactions à l'effort de guerre en A.O.F. 1914-1919*. Paris: Publications de la Sorbonne, 1982.

Miller, Charles. *Battle for the Bundu: The First World War in East Africa*. New York: Macmillan Co., 1974.

Miquel, Pierre. *La Paix de Versailles et l'opinion publique française*. Paris: Flammarion, 1972.

Moberly, F.J. *Official History of the War: Military Operations Togoland and the Cameroons, 1914-1916*. London: His Majesty's Stationery Office, 1931.

Morel, E.D. *Africa and the Peace of Europe*. London: National Labour Press, 1917.

Newitt, Malyn. *Portugal in Africa: The Last Hundred Years*. London: Longman, 1981.

Nicolson, Harold. *Peacemaking 1919*. New York: Grosset and Dunlap, 1965.

Oliphant, Sir Lancelot. *An Ambassador in Bonds*. London: Putnam and Co., 1946.

Omu, Fred I.A. *Press and Politics in Nigeria, 1880-1937*. London: Longman, 1978.

Osuntokun, Akinjide. *Nigeria in the First World War*. London: Longman, 1979.

Page, Melvin E., ed. *Africa and the First World War*. New York: St. Martin's Press, 1987.

Palo, Michael Francis. "The Diplomacy of Belgian War Aims during the First World War." Ph.D. Dissertation: University of Illinois at Urbana-Champaign, 1977.

Persell, Stuart. *The French Colonial Lobby 1889-1938*. Stanford: Hoover Institution Press, 1983.

Platt, C.M. *Finance, Trade and Politics in British Foreign Policy 1815-1914*. Oxford: Clarendon Press, 1968.

Poincaré, Raymond. *Au service de la France*. Vol. 11. *A la recherche de la paix, 1919*. Paris: Librairie Plon, 1969.

Robinson, Ronald and Gallagher, John with Denny, Alice. *Africa and the Victorians: The Climax of Imperialism*.

New York: St. Martin's Press, 1961; reprint edition, Garden City, N.Y.: Anchor Books, 1968.

Roskill, Stephen. *Hankey: man of secrets.* 3 vols. London: Collins, 1970-74.

Roux, Edward. *Time Longer than Rope.* 2nd ed. Madison: University of Wisconsin Press, 1964.

Rudin, Harry R. *Armistice 1918.* New Haven: Yale University Press, 1944; reprint edition, Hamden, Conn.: Archon Books, 1967.

_____. *Germans in the Cameroons 1884-1914.* New Haven: Yale University Press, 1938; reprint edition, Hamden, Conn.: Archon Books, 1968.

Schwabe, Klaus. *Woodrow Wilson, Revolutionary Germany, and Peacemaking, 1918-1919: Missionary Diplomacy and the Realities of Power.* Translated by Rita and Robert Kimber. Chapel Hill: University of North Carolina Press, 1985.

Scott, James Brown, supervised preparation. *Official Statements of War Aims and Peace Proposals: December 1916 to November 1918.* Washington, D.C.: Carnegie Endowment for International Peace, 1921.

Shepperson, George and Price, Thomas. *Independent African: John Chilembwe and the Origins, Setting and Significance of Nyasaland Native Rising of 1915.* Edinburgh: Edinburgh University Press, 1958.

Smith, Gaddis. "The British Government and the Disposition of the German Colonies in Africa, 1914-1919," In *Britain and Germany in Africa: Imperial Rivalry and Colonial Rule.* Edited by Prosser Gifford and William Roger Louis. New Haven: Yale University Press, 1967.

Smith, Woodruff D. *The German Colonial Empire.* Chapel Hill: University of North Carolina Press, 1978.

Smuts, J.C. *The League of Nations: A Practical Suggestion.* London: Hodder and Stoughton, 1918.

_____. *Selections from the Smuts Papers.* Vol. 3. Edited by W.K. Hancock and Jean van der Poel. Cambridge: Cambridge University Press, 1966.

Stengers, Jean. "The Congo Free State and the Belgian Congo Before 1914." In *Colonialism in Africa 1870-1960.* Vol. 1. *The History and Politics of Colonialism 1870-1914.* Edited by L.H. Gann and Peter Duignan. Cambridge: Cambridge University Press, 1969.

Stevenson, David. *French War Aims against Germany 1914-1919.* Oxford: Clarendon Press, 1982.

Stoecker, Helmuth. "The expansionist policy of imperialist Germany in Africa south of the Sahara, 1908-1918." *Etudes Africaines, African Studies, Africa-Studien.* Leipzig: Karl Marx Universitat, 1967.

Tillman, Seth P. *Anglo-American Relations at the Paris Peace Conference of 1919.* Princeton: Princeton University Press, 1961.

Townsend, Mary. *The Rise and Fall of Germany's Colonial Empire 1884-1918.* New York: Macmillan Co., 1930.

Wade, Rex. *The Russian Search For Peace, February-October 1917.* Stanford: Stanford University Press, 1969.

Walshe, Peter. *The Rise of African Nationalism in South Africa: The African National Congress, 1912-1952.* Berkeley and Los Angeles: University of California Press, 1971.

Walworth, Arthur. *America's Moment, 1918: American Diplomacy at the End of World War I.* New York: W.W. Norton and Co., 1977.

_____. *Wilson and His Peacemakers: American Diplomacy at the Paris Peace Conference, 1919.* New York: W.W. Norton and Co., 1986.

214

Watson, David. *Georges Clemenceau: A Political Biography.* London: Eyre Methuen, 1974.

Weston, Frank D.D. *The Black Slaves of Prussia.* London: Universities Mission to Central Africa, 1918.

Wheeler, Douglas L. *Republican Portugal: A Political History 1910-1926.* Madison: University of Wisconsin Press, 1978.

Wheeler-Bennett, John W. *Brest-Litovsk: The Forgotten Peace, March 1918.* London: Macmillan and Co., 1938.

Willequet, Jacques. "Anglo-German Rivalry in Belgium and Portuguese Africa." In *Britain and Germany in Africa: Imperial Rivalry and Colonial Rule.* Edited by Prosser Gifford and William Roger Louis. New Haven: Yale University Press, 1967.

_____. *Le Congo Belge et la Weltpolitik.* Brussels: Université libre de Bruxelles, 1962.

Winkler, Henry R. *The League of Nations Movement in Great Britain, 1914-1919.* New Brunswick, N.J.: Rutgers University Press, 1952.

Wright, Quincy. *Mandates under the League of Nations.* Chicago: University of Chicago Press, 1930.

Zimmermann, Emil. *The German Empire of Central Africa.* London: Longmans, Green and Co., 1918.

Articles

Andrew, C.M., Grupp, P. and Kanya-Forstner, A.S. "Le mouvement colonial français et ses principales personnalités, 1890-1914." *Revue française d'histoire d'Outre Mer* 62 (1975): 640-673.

Andrew, C.M., and Kanya-Forstner, A.S. "France, Africa and the First World War." *Journal of African History* 19 (1978): 11-23.

_____. "The French Colonial Party and French Colonial War Aims, 1914-1918." *Historical Journal* 17 (1974): 79-106.

_____. "The Groupe Colonial in the French Chamber of Deputies, 1892-1932." *Historical Journal* 17 (1974): 837-866.

Austen, Ralph A. "Duala versus Germans in Cameroon: economic dimensions of a political conflict," *Revue française d'histoire d'Outre Mer* 64 (1977): 477-497.

Bandar, Ingram. "Sidney E. Mezes and the Inquiry." *Journal of Modern History* 11 (1939): 199-202.

Coleman, James. "Togoland." *International Conciliation* 509 (September 1956).

Contee, Clarence G. "Du Bois, the NAACP, and the Pan-African Congress of 1919." *Journal of Negro History* 57, 1 (January 1972): 13-28.

Crozier, Andrew J. "The Establishment of the Mandates System 1919-25: Some Problems Created by the Paris Peace Conference." *Journal of Contemporary History* 14 (1979): 483-513.

Curry, George. "Woodrow Wilson, Jan Smuts and the Versailles Settlement." *American Historical Review* 66 (July 1961): 968-986.

Elango, Lovett. "The Anglo-French 'Condominium' in Cameroon, 1914-1916: The Myth and the Reality." *International Journal of African Historical Studies* 18, 4 (1985): 656-673.

Essiben, Madiba. "La France et la redistribution des territoires du Cameroun (1914-1916)." *Afrika Zamani* 12 and 13 (December 1981): 36-52.

Grupp, Peter. "Le 'parti colonial' français pendant la première guerre mondiale. Deux tentatives de programme commun." *Cahiers d'études Africaines* 54, 14 (1974): 377-391.

Haas, Ernest B. "The Reconciliation of Conflicting Colonial Policy Aims: Acceptance of the League of Nations Mandate System." *International Organization* 6, 4 (November 1952): 521-536.

Helmreich, Jonathan E. "Belgian Concern over Neutrality and British Intentions, 1906-1914." *Journal of Modern History* 36 (December 1964): 416-427.

Hess, Robert L. "Italy and Africa: Colonial Ambitions in the First World War." *Journal of African History* 4 (1963): 105-126.

Hodges, G.W.T. "African Manpower Statistics for the British Forces in East Africa, 1914-1918," *Journal of African History* 19 (1978): 101-116.

Hyam, Ronald. "The Partition of Africa." Review article of *Africa and the Victorians. Historical Journal* 7 (1974): 154-169.

Kennedy, Paul. "Imperial Cable Communications and Strategy, 1870-1914." *English Historical Review* 86 (October 1971): 728-752.

Kiwanuka, M. Semakula. "Colonial Policies and Administrations in Africa: The Myths of the Contrasts." *African Historical Studies* 3 (1970): 295-315.

Landes, David. "Some Thoughts on the Nature of Economic Imperialism." *Journal of Economic History* 21 (December 1961): 496-512.

Louis, William Roger. "Great Britain and the African Peace Settlement of 1919." *American Historical Review* 71 (April-July 1966): 875-892.

_____. "The United States and the African Peace Settlement of 1919: The Pilgrimage of George Louis Beer." *Journal of African History* 4 (1963): 413-433.

Lüthy, Herbert. "India and East Africa: Imperial Partnership at the End of the First World War." *Journal of Contemporary History* 6 (1971): 55-85.

Miller, David Hunter. "The Origin of the Mandates System." *Foreign Affairs* 6 (January 1928): 277-289.

Overton, John. "War and Economic Development: Settlers in Kenya, 1914-1918." *Journal of African History* 27 (1986): 79-103.

Page, Melvin E. "The War of *Thangata* : Nyasaland and the East African Campaign, 1914-1918." *Journal of African History* 19, 1 (1978): 87-100.

Platt, D.C.M. "Economic Factors in British Policy during the 'New Imperialism.'" *Past and Present* 39 (April 1968): 120-138.

Potter, Pitman B. "Origin of the System of Mandates under the League of Nations." *American Political Science Review* 16 (November 1922): 563-583.

Renouvin, Pierre. "Les buts de guerre du gouvernement français, 1914-1918." *Revue Historique* 235 (January-March, 1966): 1-38.

Savage, Donald C. and Munro, J. Forbes. "Carrier Corps Recruitment in the British East Africa Protectorate 1914-1918." *Journal of African History* 7 (1966): 313-342.

Snell, John L. "Document: Wilson on Germany and the Four-teen Points." *Journal of Modern History* 26 (December 1954): 364-369.

Stevenson, David. "French War Aims and the American Challenge, 1914-1918." *Historical Journal* 22 (1979): 877-894.

Thomas, Mary Elizabeth. "Anglo-Belgian Military Relations and the Congo Question, 1911-1913." *Journal of Modern History* 25 (June 1953): 157-165.

Warhurst, P.R. "Smuts and Africa: a study in sub-imperialism." *South African Historical Journal* 16 (1984): 82-100.

Index

Z

Plank, William G.

GULAG 65

A Humanist Looks at Aging

New York, Bern, Frankfurt/M., Paris, 1989. VIII, 205 pp.

American University Studies: Series 11, Anthropology and Sociology. Vol. 25
ISBN 0-8204-0784-4   hardback US $ 35.30/sFr. 49.50

Recommended prices - alterations reserved

Modern society, having evolved in the absence of a large cohort of the aged, has developed institutions inimical to their wellbeing. Their lives follow the Industrial-Christian model of worksacrifice-reward. Their educations provide them with work skills but not the human resources to preserve their identity in retirement, even while retirement becomes an ideology. Gerontology presides over the gerontologization of America, wherein real wealth and security are replaced by symbols. The aged, challenging the values of society, thus become a class of subversives in an extermination camp.

Contents: An analysis of how the underlying philosophical assumptions of modern society have produced an atmosphere dangerous to the survival of the aged and retired.

PETER LANG PUBLISHING, INC.
62 West 45th Street
USA - New York, NY 10036